Revising Your Résumé

CAREER BLAZERS

CAREER BOOKS FROM WILEY PRESS

Revising Your Résumé

CAREER BLAZERS

Nancy Schuman, *Vice President*
William Lewis, *President*
Career Blazers, Inc.

John Wiley & Sons, Inc.

New York · Chichester · Brisbane · Toronto · Singapore

Publisher: Stephen Kippur
Editor: Elizabeth G. Perry
Managing Editor: Katherine Schowalter
Production Services: Roberta Landi
Design: Laura Ferguson

Library of Congress Cataloging-in-Publication Data

Schuman, Nancy.
    Revising your resume.

    "A Wiley Press book."
    1. Résumés (Employment)   I. Lewis, William,
1946-   . II. Title.
HF5383.S33   1986   650.1'4   85-32320
ISBN 0-471-62485-3 (clo.)
ISBN 0-471-84523-X (ppr.)

Printed in the United States of America

   87 10 9 8 7 6 5 4

For Jane, whose résumé keeps improving

ACKNOWLEDGMENTS

THE authors gratefully acknowledge the support and contributions of the following people:

- The Placement Counselors of Career Blazers Agency who forwarded their collections of résumés, both good and bad, for use in this book.
- The staff of Career Blazers Learning Center for offering advice, input and words of encouragement.
- Elizabeth Perry, editor, whose commitment, cooperation and extraordinary patience held this project together.

CONTENTS

INTRODUCTION

Good vs. Great

WHETHER you are a recent college graduate or a seasoned executive, in all probability you possess a résumé. Résumés have become an important part of today's job-hunting process; those who don't have a résumé to offer a prospective employer are making a major business gaffe. So then, if you have a great résumé will it guarantee you a job? No, but it is likely to impress an employer and inspire him/her to interview you.

The average job-seeker possesses a *good* résumé. The job-seeker who is granted the interview possesses a *great* résumé. To the inexperienced eye the difference is minimal. To the sophisticated eye of the company recruiter or any experienced employer, the difference between good and great can be enormous.

Our objective in writing this book is not to be like all the other résumé books on the market. We're not going to help you write a résumé from scratch; we are going to show you how to *improve* the one you already have. Much of this book is common sense...no tricks or surprises. However, we can offer you our company's history of almost 40 years of wading through masses of résumés. At Career Blazers, it is our job to review résumés of potential job candidates and determine who should then be passed on to our corporate clientele. We receive over 250 unsolicited résumés weekly at our New York City headquarters.

We see good, we see bad — we even see great — but the majority of résumés that pass our desks can be improved upon. More often than not, we are surprised (sometimes shocked) at the apparent lack of savvy and care that job-seekers display regarding their résumés. Sometimes the résumé text needs rewording... or it lacks visual appeal... perhaps a more attractive typeface... or greater focus is needed in tying in experience and skills. We've learned that job-hunters can be incredibly naive when it comes to preparing a résumé.

We want to educate you — we want to offer you "résumé savvy"! To do this we have read and reread scores of résumés and decided on 60 key rules for writing a great résumé. Where appropriate, we've supplied you with samples and excerpts from real résumés (names, employers, locations, and dates have been changed to insure privacy). Read this book with your résumé in hand. Learn what you are doing right and what part of your résumé needs improvement. A checklist has been included for your convenience.

Getting a new job takes energy, time, commitment, and "smarts." A good résumé is only one part of this process, but an effective well-written résumé may allow you to "select," rather than "settle" from among a wide choice of job openings.

The Purpose of a Résumé

A résumé will never get you a job. It will, however, get you one step closer to a job by getting the interview. Your résumé's sole purpose in life is to shout at the employer and demand him/her to take action.

Your résumé is "you" in a nutshell. If you believe you have something positive to offer an employer, your résumé *must* convey that. Very often a résumé reflects how a person feels about himself/herself and employers use a résumé to gauge an individual's attitude, professionalism, and sense of self. Take your résumé seriously — especially if you want the employer to take you seriously.

The 45-Second Commercial

A great résumé makes an immediate positive visual impact on its reader. It must, since it often has a short lifespan. The average résumé reader gives no more than 30-45 seconds to sum up whether a résumé warrants further attention. If you were promoting an exciting new product to a line of fussy buyers, you would want to be certain that the product's advertising campaign captured interest. Your résumé is a marketing tool; it sells you. Therefore, show yourself off to your best advantage. Make your reader want to sit back and savor every line of your text. You want to entice the reader just enough to want more, so tell your story, but don't give away too much. Save it for a face-to-face interview!

Résumés are not easy to write. They take time, thought, and creative energy. If you're looking for a quick-and-easy formula, you won't find it here. Neither will you find a safe, simple format. Just as no two individuals are the same, no two résumés should be the same. As long as you—the job-seeker—stay within the confines of business etiquette, let your résumé reflect your own individuality. If all résumés looked alike, there would be almost no reason to have them.

Go get your résumé and see how it measures up to our rules. Be open-minded. Rather than scoff and say how great your résumé is, look for at least eight ways to improve it. A better résumé can only improve your chances for success in a highly competitive job market.

Good luck. Now...on to greatness!

R U L E 1

Decide on a format.

Chronological, Functional, or Combination

DOES your résumé fall into one of these categories?

The *chronological* résumé is the most well-known and widely used. It calls for the subject's most recent information/ experience to be listed first and then moves backward. Data are highlighted, and the writer must be aware of any obvious gaps in one's work history. Employers respond well to the chronological format because it allows them to easily review the candidate's career progress from one step to the next.

The *functional* résumé places important emphasis on the individual's overall skills and abilities. The work history is defined by specific examples and responsibilities. Dates are omitted; previous positions may or may not be included.

The *combination* approach has gained wide appeal within the last few years. It not only stresses the candidate's transferrable skills (talents that may be used at a variety of jobs), but pinpoints job titles, dates, and past employers. This style is particularly good for the entry-level to mid-career candidate because it offers both direction and depth of experience.

Excerpt From a Chronological Résumé

February 1983-
December 1985

Senior Associate Editor, *Gloss* magazine. Copy edited all copy; proofread; originated editorial ideas; acquired articles; wrote short articles, titles, captions, and blurbs; supervised other editors; worked with outside writers and columnists; served as liaison between editorial and legal departments; researched nonfiction articles (included fact-checking and source-checking); handled reader inquiries; purchased manuscripts for monthly feature; speced type on manuscripts; serialized best-sellers for publication; purchased book rights (first and second) from major book publishers; assumed duties of managing editor in his absence, including trafficking and reading boards; responsible for editorial design, concept, and implementation of major series article.

July 1981-
February 1983

Managing Editor, Human Sciences Press. Managing editor of six quarterly journals. Responsibilities included copy editing; proofreading; budget preparation; preparing print runs; supervising free-lance editorial and art staff; type specing; trafficking; scheduling; handling all forms of correspondence; serving as liaison between editors, authors, and publication staff.

Excerpt From a Functional Résumé

Accomplishments:

Marketing
— collected, analyzed and interpreted market data utilized in forecasting target companies.
— designed specific marketing campaigns and assisted in the creation of all collateral materials.
— evaluated the cost effectiveness of all marketing programs.
— determined future market strategies, both short- and long-term.

Sales
— developed and expanded sales territories by building on existing accounts and acquiring new ones.
— interacted with high-level executives at Fortune 500 corporations and negotiated sales packages agreeable to both parties.

R U L E 2

Include relevant information in your header.

IF you've forgotten the basics, a résumé will do absolutely nothing for you. Header information is composed of:

- Name
- Address (street, state, and zip code)
- Home phone number (include area code)
- Business or message phone number

So obvious, right? Well, we've seen literally hundreds of résumés where phone numbers were accidentally omitted. Few employers even bother to contact a candidate by mail. Don't make it hard for your reader to find you! A forgotten phone number may eliminate you from consideration almost immediately.

When you do write your header, keep it clean and simple. Avoid garish typefaces or fancy borders. Some information that should never be a part of your header material (or even included on your résumé) is:

- The words, "Résumé Of..."
- The date of your résumé at the time of writing
- A photograph of yourself

Sample Headers

NAME

29 Babcock Terrace • Dallas, Texas   75234
Home: (214) 555-0000   Office: (214) 555-0000

Name
662 North River Drive
Philadelphia, Pennsylvania   19104
Home: (215) 555-0000
Messages: (215) 555-0000

Note: Answering machines have enabled job-hunters to receive messages from employers that they might otherwise have missed. Take a moment to listen to your own particular message. Cute or silly is okay for friends, but don't attempt to entertain a prospective employer. Keep your message as professional as possible.

RULE 3

If you choose to include a career objective, it should be specific and give your résumé focus.

THE career objective is occasionally disguised as the job objective, career goal, work aspiration, or professional goal. Employers heatedly disagree over its inclusion on a résumé. Many find that it detracts from a résumé's overall appeal and feel it is too restrictive or confining. Some employers confess that, based on an objective, they sometimes eliminate a candidate that they might otherwise have considered. As one personnel recruiter put it, "better left unsaid, than read!"

Some job-seekers *are* comfortable stating an objective. On the positive side, it can give a résumé definition and focus. If you want to write a good career objective, be sure you do not include the words *I* or *me* in your text. The objective is always placed at the top of the résumé below the header information. If you can't write an objective that targets your interests on a position, skill, or field, we suggest that you move the objective to your cover letter. (The cover letter always accompanies the résumé when it is mailed to employers.)

Common problems associated with the objective include:

- wordiness
- narcissism
- overused (cliché)

In our search for a well-written career objective, we found that it is much easier to find a poor objective than a good one.

Examples

The following objectives are clearly defined and expressed in a positive manner, and are good examples. They stress what the employer will *get* rather than what the writer *wants*.

Professional Objective:	To work hard and learn the basics in the field of Advertising with an opportunity to develop writing skills for producing print or broadcast media.

* * *

Objective: *Employee Relations Generalist* position in a company seeking an individual with experience in the administration of salary policies, personnel policies and procedures, benefits orientations, and the development of communications programs.

* * *

PROFESSIONAL OBJECTIVE

A challenging and responsible position in which exceptional Marketing skills and a proven "track record" in Sales/Marketing would be of value. The ideal position would involve dealing with major accounts in order to service both existing and future needs, including making presentations.

The following objectives do not add to the subject's image, and are bad examples. Either trite or me-oriented, the job-seeker would be more effective working these phrases into a cover letter. Too often the objective says nothing, rather than something!

Career Objective:
An executive marketing position that thrives on independent responsibilities, individual thinking, and rewards self-motivation with substantial personal and financial rewards.

* * *

PROFESSIONAL OBJECTIVE:
To achieve a professional position with diversified responsibilities that will permit rapid professional advancement as well as personal growth.

To gain employment in an industry that enables me to use my experience and administrative abilities, yet provides an opportunity for me to reach my career goals of a more challenging and responsible position with the opportunity for greater financial growth.

* * *

Since graduating from college in 1980, I have had a fast-track career with one of the country's fastest growing Fortune 500 service companies. Recognized for my management and trouble-shooting capabilities, I have handled some of the company's most difficult assignments involving the turnaround of ineffective operational units. I am currently looking for a challenging opportunity with a progressive company that requires young, professional management.

* * *

objective
- **"Problem Solver"** A position that would enable me to combine my design, administrative, and illustration skills to solve a wide variety of problems.

R U L E 4

**If you opt to include a capsule résumé,
it should focus on the key points of the résumé
so that specific work experience and
relevant achievements are highlighted.**

THE capsule résumé is often called "Summary of Experience" or "Qualifications." It is a four- or five-line paragraph that leads off the body copy of the résumé. Its inclusion allows the reader a short introduction to the candidate's overall skills, so that he/she may then skim the body copy to find pertinent information. A capsule résumé is most effective for mid-level to senior executives.

The easiest way to write a capsule résumé is to imagine that you have less than one minute to verbally summarize your career, including key accomplishments. Then transfer your spoken words to paper. You'll find that this is much more difficult than it sounds. Most résumé writers tend to use excessive verbiage when writing their qualifications; a great capsule résumé is concise and to the point.

Poor Examples

Don't confuse a capsule with an objective. The following summary tries to do too much. Also, the pronoun *I* should not be used.

With a solid background and 15 years of experience in program development, training, and communications, I now seek to affiliate with a dynamic, growth-oriented organization. The position I desire will offer challenge, variety, responsibility, and commensurate rewards, and will utilize my abilities to communicate and manage. I have a strong need to be creative in my work and to derive a sense of accomplishment from it.

QUALIFIED FOR POSITIONS IN:

- Advertising
- Marketing Support
- Sales Promotion
- Corporate Communications
- Public Relations
- Events Coordination
- Program Development
- Community Relations

This next summary is too vague. It generalizes, but doesn't lead the reader to key points.

SUMMARY

- A lively and circumspect thinker with exposure to a broad spectrum of public policy issues;
- An efficient manager with a history of oversight responsibilities for multiple major grants;
- An effective leader who has worked with colleagues in diverse fields—e.g., the federal government, community agencies and voluntary associations, foundations, the academy, and Wall Street.

The following capsule is completely unnecessary. The subject has some valid strengths, but they would best be incorporated into a cover letter. A capsule résumé must say something about the individual's work experience and career highlights.

QUALIFICATIONS

Ability to initiate and organize projects, set priorities, and follow through with both routine and special tasks. Exercise judgment and tact while dealing with management and clients. Excellent oral and written communication skills.

Good Examples

Qualifications   Over eight years of progressive supervisory and management experience served in domestic and overseas assignments in the recreation services/ urban planning field. Primary capabilities include project management, supervision in excess of 100 personnel, budget planning and control, facility and resource management, negotiation, contract development and administration, cost analysis, and strategic planning.

* * *

FINANCIAL OFFICER/CONTROLLER

Creative problem solver adept at recognizing and developing profit potentials. Proficient in cash flow improvement, asset management, financial planning and analysis. Skilled in MIS applications, cost and general accounting systems. Experienced in financings and leveraged buyouts. MBA.

* * *

SUMMARY: Seventeen years of executive secretarial and office administration experience in the fields of insurance brokerage, law, accounting, and textiles. Have capacity to undertake independent assignments and to follow through with exacting detail on business research projects. Possess excellent writing and editing skills.

R U L E 5

The "meat" of a résumé is the
individual's work experience.
This should include effective job descriptions
with titles and names of employers.

EMPLOYERS want to see what you've done so that they can
determine if your talents and capabilities are appropriate to their
organization. Think about the responsibilities you have and how
an average day on the job measures up. Your résumé should give
the reader an accurate idea of your workload.

Begin your work experience with your job title or employer's
name. Street address is not necessary; the city and state will
suffice. Work backward — your present or most current position
first. Offer the reader dates to verify your length of service.

Allow the reader the opportunity to take in your strengths and
abilities in a glance.

Poor Examples

Production Coordinator   Jan. '83–Present

Responsibilities include:
Cost analysis of various means of production. Hiring and supervising production crews and acting as liaison between producer and
crew. Establishing accounts with suppliers and sub-contractors.
Arranging rental contracts and procurement of materials and
equipment. Supervising purchase of props. Coordinating all phases
of production.

In the previous example, the employer is not listed, and the words *Responsibilities include* should be eliminated. The tense of the text should be changed to read, "Hire and supervise production crews; act as liaison between producer and crew."

Receptionist/Secretary
- Answered phones for Media Department.
- Greeted clients and representatives.
- Typed memoranda and light correspondence.

In the above example, the employer's name and location have been omitted, and dates are missing. The writer should be more specific: What is his/her typing speed? What kind of switchboard was operated? Did he/she maintain a calendar for anyone in the office? How many people were in the Media Department?

In the following example, a description of responsibilities and length of employment would add credibility to this title. This work experience, the *meat* that is critical to the reader, is missing.

August 1966-September 1969:
L.W. Singer—Division of Random House, N.Y.
Production Associate

In the next example, the format is poor; use of columns make the résumé difficult to read. The full address is not necessary. Dates are omitted, and duties vague.

Work Experience

U.S. Environmental Protection Agency Library Clerk
Library Headquarters Responsible for a
401 M Street, SW variety of technical
Washington, DC 20460 service duties
Typing, filing, mail.

Good Examples

Spectrum, Inc., Compton, California   1982–1983
Marketing Researcher
Researched consumer market preferences and behavioral patterns.
Prepared reports and performed deadline writing.
Designed, implemented, and analyzed questionnaires.
Developed and presented forecasts and assumptions to support proposed product promotions.

* * *

1975 to 1977   **Downeast Housing, Brunswick, Maine**
                    Homebuilder and Designer
                    Supervised 37-man crew in the construction of federally funded housing programs for low-income families. Emphasis was on building with innovative design applications. Also responsible for the creation of alternate energy systems for use in conjunction with these programs.

* * *

May 1982–   NATIONAL ENDOWMENT FOR THE ARTS
April 1983   WASHINGTON, D.C.
                    The NEA is a federal agency that supports American art and artists.

                    Special Assistant to the Chairman
                    Analyzed policy and budgetary issues across the range of agency activities. Supervised the NEA's six regional representatives. Interviewed candidates for key staff positions. Acted as liaison between the Chairman and other agencies and the White House.

Work History:

Oct. 1980-
Present

**Assistant Program Director,
Society for Seamen's Children,
Staten Island, New York**
Aid in the coordination and supervision of social work staff in a child welfare agency. Responsibilities include: program planning, staffing, public relations, negotiating, directing, and decision making. Duties include: administrative components, assisting in management of program budget, presentations, conducting case conferences and unit meetings. Other duties are: liaison work with collateral agencies, eligibility determination, and crisis intervention.

R U L E 6

Use action verbs to describe
your responsibilities.

ASK any employer what kind of candidate he/she looks for, and we know the response will be: "A *doer*." The job-seeker with a résumé that implies action, assertiveness, and a take-charge manner will cause immediate interest.

In order to convey your readiness and willingness to plunge wholeheartedly into a prospective employer's new duties, tell your readers what you have accomplished in other positions. Do this with strong words—words that accurately reflect your abilities.

As you use action verbs to describe your responsibilities, be careful to be accurate and truthful. Some job-seekers get caught up in the need to sound like "Super Candidate," and their use of strong words sound exaggerated and unnecessary. As one personnel director told us, "I can immediately tell when a person is inflating his responsibilities. The résumé stops reading like a résumé and turns into an advertisement for a big ego. I'm not impressed."

Here is a list of verbs to help you describe your job duties and achievements.

adapted	delegated	interviewed	purchased
administered	demonstrated	investigated	recommended
allocated	designed	launched	recruited
amended	developed	lectured	reduced
analyzed	devised	led	reinforced
appointed	directed	maintained	reorganized
approved	drafted	managed	researched
arbitrated	edited	marketed	reviewed
assigned	elminated	modified	revised
assisted	established	monitored	scheduled
audited	evaluated	motivated	selected
budgeted	expanded	negotiated	solved
built	expedited	organized	streamlined
calculated	forecasted	participated	strengthened
cataloged	formulated	performed	structured
collected	founded	pinpointed	supervised
communicated	generated	planned	supported
compiled	guided	prepared	taught
computed	headed	processed	trained
conducted	implemented	promoted	translated
controlled	increased	proposed	trimmed
coordinated	initiated	provided	unified
created	interpreted	published	wrote

Writing quality job descriptions is no easy task. It is difficult to tell our readers how and where to draw the line. The phrasing of your responsibilities must sound assertive, yet sincere. Perhaps the best way to explain what we mean is to give you examples from individuals who either hit or missed the mark. We think you'll be able to begin discerning the fine line between good and great.

The Misses

PINPOINTED areas of interest and obtained crucial information from target markets, utilizing surveys that indicated product preferences and attracted advertisers.

This one is very close to being great. The use of capital letters hurts more than helps. The overemphasis of action comes off a bit like bragging, rather than description. It is our opinion that a little toning down would make this excerpt a real success!

CONCEIVED and executed innovative promotional strategies, designing a logo and distributing a spectrum of other items, culminating in organizational identity and high visibility.

REVITALIZED a founding organization by expanding its communications, teaching workshop methods to selected representatives, and applying effective sales techniques to stimulate acceptance nationwide.

REPRESENTED the organization through personal appearances at local, state and national conferences, demonstrating thorough product knowledge to spark public awareness.

GENERATED more than $250,000 for a special project over two years by cultivating rapport with corporations, foundations, and individuals, providing the wherewithal for an on-going program.

OPTIMIZED the use of print and electronic media, writing and placing effective press releases to ensure favorable coverage and image enhancement.

EMPLOYED computerization to refine operations and streamline the work flow, achieving dramatic time savings while reducing annual costs by $30,000.

RESTRUCTURED an entire operation and defined functions, manualizing procedures and prioritizing tasks, resulting in a 50% increase in productivity.

The writer of the following is obviously a good communicator. However, we dislike the way the "Facts" are presented. Less gimmick and a more conservative tone would have enhanced this individual's assets.

FACT: My marketing strategies have helped launch two successful enterprises, taking them from dubious grass roots to profitable green pastures.

FACT: Negotiating with senior executives and corporate heads is second nature to me.

FACT: My insatiable independent, entrepreneurial drive and fidelic commitment make direct office supervision not only redundant but mutually unprofitable.

FACT: Academically, a 3.75 undergraduate G.P.A. speaks for itself; a Master's degree calls out the facts; nine credits towards my Ph.D shout.

FACT: I consider communications—verbal, written, publications—to be an art...I consider myself an artist.

The Hits

MANUFACTURERS HANOVER TRUST CO., NY, NY   8/81–10/84
Assistant Secretary, Operations Support Services

Responsible for personnel and operational budget of $5 million. Directed official and managerial staff of 14, plus 125 clericals. Responsible for all production and customer service.

- Set up management by objective goals thereby reducing accounts receivable "cost to carry" from $3000 to $1000 per day.
- Developed new procedures which reduced customer inquiries 40%.
- Reduced production daily error ratio from 7% to 1% utilizing new training program.
- Installed automated system for mailing charges which cut expenses 30% annually.
- Eliminated daily liabilities and reduced aged liabilities from 280 to 9.
- Appointed committee member of four professional business associations.

Human Resources

Personnel Intern, American Standard Inc., New York, NY, summer, winter, 1983. Assisted in implementation of new human resource system; documented user's guide. Classified résumés, wrote newsletters, job descriptions, and litigation summaries. Prepared compensation reports based on Hay point system. Assisted in formulation of EEO report. Gained knowledge of affirmative action, interviewing, training, benefits, and classification of exempt/nonexempt employees.

* * *

June 1981 to Present

Warwick & Finney, Inc., Chicago, Illinois

Finance Assistant

— *Assist payroll/billing manager with 500+ member temporary employee payroll*
— *Field all employee questions regarding timesheets, paychecks, W-2s and W-4s, hours accumulated, and address changes*
— *Issue stop payments on checks as needed; coordinate procedures with bank officers, and manage follow-through on replacement checks*
— *Process and microfilm employee timesheets; dispatch film to 3M*
— *Prepare daily cash/accounts received; enter data into ledger book*
— *Handle all accounting department typing, including invoices and correspondence; basic keyboard knowledge (40 wpm typing) and familiarity with CRT and VT-100*
— *Manage capital and supply inventories for entire department; place orders with vendors and maintain purchase records*

RULE 7

Tie in skills and experience
relevant to the job objective.

THE key word in this rule is *relevant*. It is not enough to simply list every job you've had since high school or college graduation; you have to show that the experiences you have had coincide with the employer's needs. Whether you actually include it or not on paper, every résumé writer must know what his/her objective is in job hunting. You can't sit back and hope a good opportunity will find you. If you've thought about your interests and how what you've done has fed these interests, you should be able to communicate this on paper. Knowing what kind of position you want, and then marketing your experience on your résumé, tells an employer you are a good candidate for his/her job opening.

It is very important that you show how your past experiences and learned skills will contribute to your success with the employer's organization. Be careful to avoid the following résumé pitfalls:

- A listing of a wide range of jobs with no common thread. To the reader's eye, there must appear to be an identifiable interest or link to your career choices.
- The failure to show how each new job brought you one step closer to greater career growth and responsibility.

Two résumé excerpts follow. The first lacks cohesion; the individual appears to have chosen his/her positions at random (the reader cannot tell what ties the experiences together to build a certain expertise). The second résumé excerpt clearly shows a progressive chain of events in the subject's career development.

Poor Example

What holds these experiences together? The reader of the following must guess as to what transferrable skills enabled the subject to move from one position to the next. The writer must provide more information.

WORK EXPERIENCE

ADDAMS & TAFT, INC., Indianapolis, Indiana
Worked in corporate finance department and gained insight into investment banking. (1985)

TACT, INC., Newark, Ohio
Worked on an assembly line in plastics factory. (1984)

NORTH NEWARK LITTLE LEAGUE, Newark, Ohio
Worked as an umpire. (Summers 1977–1983)

Good Example

The subject has a clear interest in retail, as well as experience with promotional work and some advertising. There is demonstrable growth from one position to the next.

WORK EXPERIENCE

July 1981–June 1983
IRON MOUNTAIN
STONEWARE FACTORY OUTLET
Flemington, New Jersey
Assistant Manager in retail outlet. Responsibilities included review of promotional material, customer service, and interface with vendors to resolve problems.

November 1978–August 1979
MACY'S at the STATEN ISLAND MALL
Work involved purchasing, sales, and promotional work in the fine china department.

August 1977–August 1978
JEWELS BY EDWAR
Beverly Hills, California
Responsibilities encompassed advertising, retail sales, as well as training in the appraising and purchasing of fine gems and stones.

September 1971–November 1978
Extensive work as a professional actor in theater and radio/television commercials. This work required excellent communicative skills and an understanding of the inner workings of advertising agencies and mass media marketing.

RULE 8

Work experiences should emphasize skills; never list your previous duties in a bland manner—employers dislike "laundry list" résumés.

IT always surprises us when we receive a résumé that reads like a laundry list or a supermarket list of items to buy. A résumé is sent to an employer to convey information about an individual. Why then do so many résumé writers get stingy with the information they give out?

As you write or rewrite your résumé, be careful to devote time and consideration to your work experiences. Make them come alive for your reader. Let them say something positive about you and what you are capable of doing. If you present your experiences in a dull, unpleasant manner, the reader may get the very same impression of you!

Note: Job-seekers who make use of the functional or combination résumé format often list their work history at the end of the résumé, naming only employers and dates. This *is* acceptable if you have correctly handled what the functional or combination résumé is all about. These formats present a synopsis or overview of the subject's skills, talents, and achievements. Experiences and events are interwoven, so that transferrable skills are highlighted.

Poor Examples

EXPERIENCE

Business

- **RESEARCH ANALYST/LIMITED PARTNER;**
  Penn Stocks, Phila., PA
  Performed maintenance research on equity portfolio utilizing
  research techniques.   Sept. 1982–present

- **RESEARCH ASSOCIATE;**
  Wilson & Harris Associates, Phila., PA
  Conducted financial research at business information center.
  Specialized in corporate documents and SEC filings, with
  extensive client and source contact.   Nov. 1980–Aug. 1982

- **ASSISTANT MANAGER;**
  Penn Student Agencies, Travel Div., Phila., PA
  Arranged travel plans for university groups and
  organized bus tours to major cities during vacation
  periods.   Jan. 1980–Nov. 1980

- **RESEARCH ASSOCIATE/INTERN;**
  The Ward Center, Pittsburgh, PA
  Compiled and cataloged library of domestic and foreign
  annual reports.   Sept. 1978–Sept. 1980

* * *

Chevy Mens Shop
2088 86th Street
Brooklyn, NY 11214

5/79 to 6/81

Assistant Sales Manager & Buyer

Barnes & Noble
105 5th Avenue
New York, NY

5/77 to 4/79

Inventory maintenance & Sales Assistant

Good Examples

PROFESSIONAL EXPERIENCE

December
1982–
August 1984

New York State Mortgage Loan Enforcement and Administration Corporation
New York, New York
Mortgage Accountant

Monitored over 100 Public Housing complexes throughout New York State, which were set up through limited partnerships to serve as tax shelters. Audited the financial condition of these facilities. Prepared operating budgets and forecasts, as well as capital budgets. Reviewed monthly, quarterly, and year-end financial statements. Generated cash flow projections. Implemented and responsible for variance analyses. Monitored financial aspects of close to $1 billion in Public Benefit Corporation Bond Issues.

* * *

December
1975–
August 1979

Legal Assistant/Office Manager,
White, White & Griffin, Seattle, Washington

- Recruited, trained and supervised secretarial support staff.

- Analyzed office routines and implemented procedural changes to increase staff productivity.

- Developed training manuals.

- Corresponded with clients, attorneys, bankers, and executives, and scheduled meetings, conferences, and closings.

- Represented office at court calendar calls and bank closings.

- Monitored document in/out flow for timely filing and appearances in court.

- Researched docketed files in county clerks' offices.

RULE 9

Avoid long paragraphs— they are difficult to read. Job descriptions should be no longer than six to eight lines of text.

WHILE content is of primary importance, the use of long paragraphs to describe your employment experience can be visually exhausting to your reader. Long paragraphs make the reader work harder...he/she has to dig for facts.

When you use large blocks of type you may be "weighing down" your résumé. If your résumé contains large blocks of type, try to look at it objectively. Ask yourself these questions:

- Is the overall appearance attractive?
- Do the paragraphs enhance my qualifications?
- Can I edit my sentences?

Bear in mind that employers like to skim. When you use long paragraphs in your body copy, you may shorten the amount of time the employer will devote to your résumé.

Good Use of a Descriptive Paragraph

In the following example, note that the writer kept sentences short and skipped one line between key points. This helps to break up the heaviness of the text.

SAKS FIFTH AVENUE—New York

Manager of designer imports for seven months followed by promotion to manager of Bridal Salon. Excellent sales record based on personalized service and fashion know-how.

Executive responsibilities include staff supervision, weekly planning report, coordination of special events such as fashion shows and promotions, customer correspondence, phone inquiries, and various administrative duties.

Also contributed monthly to "Focus," the company newsletter featuring employee notes plus other highlights within the New York store and its branches.

Paragraphs in Need of Improvement

The following shows how the subject chose to write about his/her job description.

Handling and processing customer orders and quotations. Calculating and adjusting prices of our parts based on how much time it took to make as well as cost of material involved.

Operating Spery Univac BC/7 computer. Computer duties: Training and assisting new personnel. Processing customer orders and entering information into the computer which is relevant to our business such as Bill To and Ship To Customers, tax codes, customer codes, updating prices, as well as overseeing all input into the computer, etc. I also must know everyone's duties, who deal with the computer so I can take over their duties if they are out.

Using the above material, note the improvements.

Handle and process customer orders and quotations. Calculate and adjust prices on parts based on labor and material costs.

Operate Spery Univac BC/7 computer. Process customer data such as Bill To, Ship To, tax codes, customer codes, and price updates. Train and assist new personnel; substitute for computer staff as needed.

R U L E   1 0

Use concise phrases rather than sentences; eliminate the use of pronouns such as *I, me, my, myself,* etc.

ON a résumé, space is limited, particularly for those with lengthy careers or values experiences. Therefore, the more concise you can be, the more room you will have to include *all* of your accomplishments and experiences.

As you write your job duties and responsibilities, there is no need to form complete sentences or make use of the pronouns *I, me, my,* etc. Such pronouns are understood, rather than stated. Never refer to yourself as "the writer," or write about yourself in the third person, as in "Mary Smith organized." Use parallel sentence structure; make sure your verb tenses agree. For example, do not write "coordina*ted*" fund drive" and then switch to "hir*ing* all support staff." Your phrasing should make every word count. Tight, concise descriptions will make a strong, easy-to-read résumé.

Examples of Concise Job Descriptions

MANAGING EDITOR
August 1980– August 1983

CABLE AMERICA, CABLE ATLANTA, Atlanta Georgia. Responsibilities included: supervising, designing, editing, and layout of monthly program guides representing premium and basic services for Cable Television; program guide serves five metropolitan areas: Los Angeles, Atlanta, DeKalb, East Point, and College Park; selecting prime positional spots in the guide for advertisers to promote their products; designing and editing direct mail pieces and flyers for Cable Atlanta.

* * *

EXPERIENCE:
1980 to present

MARKETING REPRESENTATIVE, YOURDON, INC., NEW YORK, NY
Market computer software education and consulting services to top management of major companies. Maintain complete control of sales in 9 states with the achievement of a 158% increase in sales over preceding year. Majority of sales come from active participation in detailed telephone marketing program, self-initiated direct mail campaigns and live sales presentations. Assist with publicity releases and advertising strategies. Create advertisements for territorial trade journals.

In the following example the layout is weak; use of columns is poor spacing. Content and phrasing, however, are very good.

1983- R.H. Macy
1984 Herald Square
New York, NY

Assistant Buyer — Curtains
Complete financial planning of sales and stock for total department and individual stores by season. Purchasing for basic and promotional merchandise. Planning and presenting of seasonal advertising. Merchandising and display planning for Herald Square store and branch stores.

R U L E   11

Consider using bullets to set off special responsibilities.

THIS rule is a variation on the use of paragraph structure for job descriptions. Some résumé writers prefer to list distinct job responsibilities for each place of employment and then highlight these duties by the use of bullets or some similar mark. Each skill/duty is given special attention. This format is a good option for those job-seekers who might otherwise be forced to write lengthy paragraphs to detail their diverse responsibilities.

Bulleting is widely accepted by employers and is extremely easy for a reader to digest. We've included several excellent examples of individuals who were able to present their skills through the use of bullets.

Good Examples

11/78–6/80   *Editorial Assistant,* NEXT *Magazine*

- Organized entire editorial department—ordered reference books, source materials, and subscriptions; created a cross-referenced subject catalog for filed source material; collaborated with lawyer to create standard contracts for artists and writers; set up correspondence files.
- Researched story ideas—obtained source material, interviewed potential sources, reported back to editors.
- Fact-checked press-ready copy.
- Trafficked type.
- Handled own correspondence.
- Typed manuscripts and transcribed interviews.
- Acted as personal secretary to editor.
- Managed office—helped coordinate office move, ordered supplies, handled problems, etc.

* * *

Thoroughbred horse trainer—
Belmont, Aqueduct, and Saratoga

- Manager and operator of public racing stable.
- Acquired and serviced customers.
- Handled all business in regard to buying and selling.
- Supervised ten men in every aspect of operating a racing stable.
- Made all decisions in respect to where the horses will race and what their current market value is.

EXPERIENCE: **PRICE WATERHOUSE, CPA,** New York, NY
Professional Assistant, February 1985–Present

- Preparing and computing individual, sales, and use tax returns
- Analyzing work-in-progress ledgers and preparing billing analysis status report
- Researching technical tax questions for clients
- Analyzing and posting clients' monthly stock statements by journal entires
- Assisting managers and senior accountants on administrative functions
- Microcomputer experience:
  Lotus 1-2-3
  Wordstar
  Basic

* * *

1975 to Present   *Director of Building Services*
Educational Broadcasting Corporation
Channel Thirteen, Kansas City, Missouri

- Develop, coordinate, and supervise building services staff of 22
- Interview and select personnel in building services department
- Eliminate consideration of outside contractors by training personnel in order to save corporation money
- Develop and recommend budget for all building services
- Conceive fire safety plan in building
- Effectively supervise maintenance and repairs of all heating, ventilation, and air conditioning equipment at four locations
- Adeptly direct, rearrange, and renovate lighting, plumbing, ceilings, walls, and flooring in numerous offices
- Plan and organize cleaning procedures and schedules

R U L E 1 2

Don't be afraid to use the vocabulary associated with your industry.

IF you are a job-seeker who is planning to stay within your industry, don't hesitate to use the jargon of your trade. Employers tell us that they like to see a candidate use a business buzz word to indicate credibility. We are not suggesting that you immediately begin to use technical, complex terms, but rather the vocabulary one would encounter daily in your field.

For example, legal professionals who use the term *Blue Sky*, data processing professionals who indicate their knowledge of certain computer languages, and advertising executives who use lingo associated with Madison Avenue. When you prepare a résumé it is perfectly acceptable to write for your audience, as long as you know *who* your audience will be. Please note that if you plan to change fields, it is best to keep language simple, direct, and easy to understand for those who may be unfamiliar with the specifics of your previous career area.

Examples Using Trade Language

Television Representatives
New York, New York

Sales Assistant

Worked with salespersons dealing with various television stations throughout the United States. Responsibilities included working with BIAS Computer System inputing demographics for reports and availabilities. Intermediary between television stations and advertising agencies. Corresponded by telephone and TWX regarding orders and contracts. This included dealing with makegoods, timing, and placements. Worked Nielsen and Arbitron.

* * *

Assistant Controller

- Maintenance of General Ledger and Subledgers.
- Bank reconciliations.
- Cash reconciliations.
- Supervision of Accounting clerk, Data Entry clerks, and CD's clerk.
- Preparation of Federal Reserve reports.

* * *

Electrical Designer-Drafter/Petro-Chemical

Responsibilities included design and documentation of all working drawings. Projects included sump installations, lighting design, equipment rack layouts, heat tracing, and instrumentation jobs relating to refinery upgrading.

* * *

SKILLS

- Motion Picture Film Editor—35mm & 16mm
- VTR Editing
- Animation Designer/Producer
- Graphic Designer—Print
- Designer/Producer—Multimedia
- Designer/Producer—Computer Graphics
- Computer-Aided Chartographics
- Knowledge of Computer Systems

* * *

COMPUTER	COBOL
LANGUAGES:	PL/I
	BASIC
	FORTRAN
	PASCAL

R U L E 1 3

Use numbers to show management responsibility and quantitative results such as reductions, increases, and profitability.

IN business, the bottom line is profit/loss. Nothing you write will be as dramatic or significant as what you say regarding your contributions to the bottom line. Employers don't want implied action—they want the cold, hard facts. This is a clear-cut opportunity to boast about your successes—to "blow your own horn," so to speak.

- How much did you save the company?
- How many people did you supervise?
- How much money were you able to collect?
- How much did you increase sales?

You'll note that the key words here are *how much* and *how many*. When you write about your accomplishments, give the reader facts. Don't make the mistake of writing abstract generalizations or passive statements. Give your readers numbers they can think about. List concrete, quantifiable information.

Examples of Dollar-Wise Job-Seeker Statements

CBS/FM National Sales
Vice President/General Manager

- Managed 29 people in 7 offices selling radio time for 32 stations.
- Forecasted and budgeted, long- and short-range.
- Increased total billings from $4.7MM to $10.6MM.
- Increased represented stations from 10 to 32.

* * *

- Contributed $200,000 to profits by restructuring procedures and controls, eliminating a major recurring inventory loss.
- Reduced container inventory requirements 15% by installing an inventory control system.
- Saved company $60,000 annually by instituting a system for investigation and collection of shortage claims.
- Contributed $100,000 to annual cash flow through major reduction in accounts receivable.
- Added $30,000 to annual net income through short-term investment of excess cash.

* * *

— *Supervised a major customer service department, which received an average of 220,000 telephone and 30,000 mail inquiries per year from health care professionals throughout New York State.*
— *Developed and implemented service and performance standards. This resulted in a 24% increase in the incoming call completion rate from 61% to 85% on a daily basis.*

* * *

SELECTED ACHIEVEMENTS

- Converted major division's $2,000,000 loss to $4,000,000 profit within three years.
- Formulated an innovated parts pricing program that increased revenues, generating, $1,000,000 in ongoing profits.
- Instituted new procedure that reduced royalty payments and recovered $500,000 in overpayments.
- Conducted manufacturing facility survey that resulted in a reallocation of resources, saving $400,000 annually.

───── R U L E   1 4 ─────

Omit "reason for leaving" a previous employer.

THE reason for leaving a previous employer is not considered appropriate information to include on a résumé. When we have seen it noted, it always seems to be on résumés where the tone is either self-pitying or "sour grapes." In other words, we have never seen a candidate write, "A golden opportunity came along!" Most include statements such as: "Company went bankrupt," "Massive lay-off," "No growth," etc. Why put anything as negative as these statements on your résumé?

If you have been laid off by an employer who has given you a letter of reference indicating your termination is through no fault of your own, do *not* attach it to your résumé. Most employers will not read it, and those who do, will do so with suspicion. Such letters are best sent directly from employer to employer.

Keep your résumé free of "reasons." If you are fortunate enough to be extended an invitation to interview, it is very likely one of the questions will be: Why have you decided to leave your present position? Save this information for a face-to-face discussion; *never do the following*!

REASON FOR   Belief that ability and training warrant higher
LEAVING: salary.

Reason for Leaving—See letter of recommendation (attached).

R U L E 1 5

Never include salary requirements or salary received on previous positions.

SALARY requirements are a résumé taboo. It is a breach of résumé etiquette to include this information. If you think about it, the inclusion of such information is likely to be more harmful than helpful. If you list a figure that is too high, the employer will immediately eliminate you from consideration. An amount that is too low may make you appear to be inexperienced or naive.

Employers will talk money when they are ready—usually on the second or third interview. Sometimes candidates think they must include a history of earnings because they are responding to a classified advertisement where this information is requested. Employers will review all the responses, not just the ones where salary information is included. You are not obligated to provide this information, and if you choose to do so, the place to do it is in your cover letter.

The following excerpts are obvious résumé errors.

SALARY
REQUIREMENTS: $16,000–$18,000 depending on nature and location of position.

Position Held—Customer Engineer

Employment Responsibilities—The repair and preventative maintenance of approx. 2,400 IBM office products, which were under service agreement with IBM.

Reason for Leaving—Felt salary was not in keeping with the additional expenses incurred in working in and commuting to Manhattan.

Salary History—Began at about $10,000 per year; progressed to about $14,000 per year.

The above excerpt is a triple taboo... "Reason for Leaving" is unnecessary; "Salary History" should be deleted; and the script typeface is inappropriate!

R U L E 1 6

Never list the name of a supervisor.

THIS rule is another résumé "don't." A supervisor's name is completely unnecessary. Prospective employers do not need to know the name of the person you reported to on your last position or any previous posts. This information is excessive. Candidates occasionally include it so that they are not asked to provide the names of references later. Let the employer ask you for this information if he/she so desires. As with an attached letter of reference, employers may suspect that the name of the supervisor is fabricated—perhaps the name of a friend or coworker. The inclusion of a supervisor's name also suggests a lack of sophistication in business. Don't let the employer catch you unaware. Your résumé should contain only relevant skills and information. Make everything on your résumé contribute to a polished, professional image of yourself.

Don't do the following!

Oct. 1976–	Social Worker,	To supervise the
Dec. 1978	Catholic Children's	placement and progress
Salary:	Aid.	of wards at private
$10,300 (app.)	Supervisor: Lee Tyler	institutions and group
		homes. To provide
		counselling to children
		and evidence at Court.

Supervisor and salary information is irrelevant; duties are vague; and the three-column format is poor use of space.

———— R U L E   1 7 ————

Beware of obvious gaps in work history. Frequent "job-hoppers" should down-play short-term employment.

ONE of the most important traits employers look for in a candidate is *stability*. If you have had many short-term positions or there are significant time gaps in your work history, you will have to do your best to keep this information from appearing as a prominent part of your résumé. Gaps, as well as frequent job-hopping, make employers nervous. You must remember that they are looking for the best possible person for the job—someone who will come in and play a key role in their organization; someone who will make a commitment. Employers do not want to hire an individual only to find that he/she leaves soon afterward due to boredom or lack of responsibility. There are ways to down-play obvious gaps or too many employers in your career. Take a good look at the advice that follows:

Create a functional or combination résumé rather than a chronological résumé. As we've explained previously, the chronological résumé emphasizes dates, often displaying this information as a prominent part of the left-hand margin. Stay clear of this format!

Place your employment dates at the end of your job description. Down-play the lack of time spent with the employer and play up the experience itself.

Classify several of your short-term positions together, as though they were one experience.

Homemakers returning to the marketplace should omit any obvious reference to their time spent at home. Do highlight any volunteer or unpaid experience within the community or local social organizations during this time period. Employers are experiencing a positive new consciousness-raising when it comes to re-entry women and their contributions in volunteer activities that closely parallel responsibilities held in today's business environment.

Poor Examples

January 1985-   Sarasota, Florida
June 1985

What was this candidate doing?

1972–1978	Homemaker. Devoted 6 years to childrearing and motherhood.
4/84–8/84	General Tours, Inc., File Clerk
8/84–12/84	Grey Advertising, Receptionist/Media Department
1/85–5/85	Homestead Products Corp., Accounts Payable Clerk

Good Examples

This next example is a rewrite of the last excerpt above.

| 1984–1985 | Temporary employment within the realm of travel/tourism, advertising, and consumer products. Assignments included: General Tours, Inc.; Grey Advertising; and Homestead Products Corp. Handled a variety of clerical support responsibilities such as reception, filing, light typing, and accounts payable. |

* * *

Council on Foreign Relations, New York, NY

Functioned as Assistant to Director of Funding. Maintained log of donations, maintained daily figure calculations, and assisted with layout of financial information for final presentation in Annual Report. (6/84–12/84)

RULE 18

**Highlight events and achievements
of your career. Where appropriate,
separate them from the job description
so that special accomplishments
receive recognition.**

THINK about your career to date. Are there any single moments or high points that stand out in your mind? Because résumés are self-advertisements, you may want to include information which, for some, represents their "finest hours." This information can add to your credibility and should clearly demonstrate to your reader that you take an active role in making things happen wherever you may be employed.

When you can offer an outstanding accomplishment, do so. Give concrete facts and figures. Employers firmly believe that someone who has tasted success will want to do so again and again.

The following excerpts exemplify this rule.

SELECTED ACCOMPLISHMENTS

Reduced direct costs $1,500,000 for six manufacturing locations by installing standard cost system.

Established department for multimillion dollar firm, saving $100,000 and increasing management information and control.

Created and developed inventory control system, facilitating production planning and increasing cash flow by $200,000.

Reorganized credit department, decreasing collection cycle and increasing cash availability by $400,000.

* * *

SPECIAL ACHIEVEMENTS

- Developed close business ties with major wire houses, e.g., Merrill Lynch; Donaldson Lufkin, Integrated Resources; Oppenheimer; E.F. Hutton.
- Closed $1 million private limited partnership for leading institutional salesmen and executives from Paine Webber.
- Formed real estate development company. Raised $5 million; acquired four major properties and commenced development of properties valued in excess of $30 million.
- Negotiated $15.3 million loan with First National Bank of Chicago to purchase 248 acres of prime waterfront property in Long Beach, California.

RULE 19

Include any awards won or industry recognition earned.

IT is important to include any special awards you've earned because they signify that you have been recognized by your peers and superiors as someone with outstanding talents and abilities. Awards may be incorporated into the employment section, or they may rate their own separate heading. Next to the award, note the time period for which you've earned this recognition. Be sure that the award's significance can be understood by your reader. For example, an award titled "The Markart Memorial" gives the reader no clue that it is issued to the individual who has achieved the greatest sales in the northeast region. Therefore, the candidate must include a succinct explanation following the award if it needs further clarification.

Sample award statements from résumés include:

- Who's Who in American Business
- Awards cited for significant publications
- Salesperson of the Month/Quarter/Year
- Million Dollar Club
- Most Valuable Performance
- Consistent Production
- Employee of the Year

R U L E   2 0

Mention professional memberships or affiliations if they add to your credibility.

MEMBERSHIPS and credentials indicate that you take an active interest in your field. They can be especially meaningful to an employer if you have held an office or taken a leadership role on a well-known group or committee. Membership experience cannot compensate for lack of significant work experience, but it does show that you have broadened your activities and have made an attempt to interact and network with others in your field.

The following excerpts illustrate this rule.

* * *

MEMBERSHIPS

Association of Independent Video and Filmmakers (AIVF); ASIFA (international animation society).

* * *

Affiliations and   International Word Processing Association
Memberships: Business Education Association
                      American Society for Training and Development

* * *

Affiliations:
    Fellow, Casualty Actuarial Society
    Member, American Academy of Actuaries
    Member, International Actuarial Association and ASTIN Section

* * *

PROFESSIONAL AFFILIATIONS
    American Society of Association Executives
    National Education Association

RULE 21

Follow the correct education format when outlining your academic history.

THE education portion of a résumé encompasses colleges attended, location (specific addresses not given), degrees (major/minor), academic concentration, honors, and related activities.

If a job-seeker has at least five years of work experience, less significance is devoted to education. Entry-level candidates and relative newcomers may opt to expand on this section for lack of employment information. Academic experience follows employment history on all résumés but those of recent graduates. A typical format follows:

> College/University, City, State
> Degree in Major; Minor
> Date of Graduation
> Academic Honors
> Activities

For example:

> Indiana University, Bloomington, IN
> B.S. in Biology, Chemistry minor
> May 1984
> Dean's List, Graduated Cum Laude
> Self-financed 100% of undergraduate expenses
> President, Health Science Club, 1984

Pay attention to details such as date of completion and your area of study. Here are two other versions of Education formats:

EDUCATIONAL EXPERIENCE

B.A. in JOURNALISM and   **Rutgers College, Rutgers**
SOCIOLOGY   **University,** New Brunswick, NJ.
September 1977–May 1981

* * *

EDUCATION   Emerson College, Boston, Massachusetts
B.S. in Mass Communications Television
Production
Minor in Psychology
May 1985

Next, we show two poor examples of résumé excerpts. In their original formats they failed to express the subject's academic experience in a positive and professional manner. We've created two *before* and *after* situations. See if you agree with our modifications.

Before

Education

Brooklyn College   Fashion Inst. of Technology
Bedford Avenue   227 West 27th Street
Brooklyn, NY   New York, NY

Major: Liberal Arts   Major: Buying & Merchandising
Term: 1 Year '79   Term: 1 Semester, '81

Kingsborough Community College
2001 Oriental Blvd.
Brooklyn, NY

Major: Business Management
Term: 1 Semester, '81

After

EDUCATION

Kingsborough Community College, Brooklyn, NY   1981
Fashion Institute of Technology, New York, NY   1981
Brooklyn College, Brooklyn, NY   1979

Coursework included: Liberal Arts, Buying & Merchandising, and Business Management
45 credits toward completion of B.S.

Before

EDUCATION: **B.S. DEGREE,** Claflin College, Orangeburg, SC

Major: Mathematics... Minor: Computer Science

Honors/Activities—Alpha Kappa Alpha Sorority—named Outstanding Member of the Year... Undergraduate Sorority Member with the Highest Academic Average... Director's Award... Who's Who Among Colleges and Universities... Most Outstanding Female Student... Dean's List... Honor Roll... Winner, Thomas Music Award. Additionally involved in Student Government Association, Pan-Hellenic Council, and Concert Choir.

Courses—Quantitative Methods... Operations Research... Statistics... Computer and Mathematics courses.

After

EDUCATION

1984   Claflin College, Orangeburg, SC
B.S. Mathematics; Computer Science Minor
Coursework: Quantitative Methods, Statistics, Operations Research, and Computers
Honors: Dean's List
Who's Who Among Colleges & Universities
Outstanding Female Student
Alpha Kappa Alpha Sorority—Member of the Year
Activities: Member, Student Government Association

R U L E 2 2

An education listing need not be long or detailed unless the subject is a recent college graduate.

EMPLOYERS are not seeking a detailed account of the four years you spent at a university. As with every segment of your résumé, an employer will review the "Education" section looking for key information that will be useful to him/her. We've included two excerpts from résumés where the candidate's education was given appropriate attention.

New graduates are cautioned *not* to expend unnecessary energy compiling academic information that will not benefit the reader. If you lack specific employment experience, do not try to compensate for it by expanding your academic experience. Where work experience is sparse, include academic internships or relevant activities as additive information.

Education	State University of New York at Albany. Major in English with minor in psychology; coursework included several electives in grammar and writing. Bachelor of Arts (magna cum laude)—May 1981.

* * *

EDUCATION:

June 1977: Brown University, Providence, RI, **Magna Cum Laude.** Bachelor of Arts degree in Semiotics, an interdisciplinary program combining literature, linguistics and film. Grade-point average: 3.75. Education partly financed by two academic scholarships. Active on university radio station and daily newspaper.

R U L E 2 3

Write out degrees
that are relatively unknown;
for widely accepted degrees
(MA, MS, MBA, BA, BS)
an abbreviation is appropriate.

A PERSONNEL recruiter recently inquired, "What is an M.H.S. degree?" We later learned that it was a Master of Human Services degree. As new academic degrees (primarily graduate) are offered by universities and colleges, a new array of degree abbreviations will be brought to the attention of the business world. Students are using interdisciplinary studies to creatively coordinate core curriculum for specialized programs. However, until these degrees become widely recognized, we suggest that you write out your degree word-for-word. If your degree is familiar to most, it is unnecessary to write it out; in fact, many employers find the explanation of standard degrees to be tedious and unsophisticated. Never include the word *degree* on your résumé.

The following examples—*before* and *after*—illustrate this rule.

Before

St. John's University, New York
Degree: Master of Business Administration, June 1984
G.P.A. 3.4
Major: Marketing Management

Bernard M. Baruch College, New York
Degree: Bachelor of Business Administration, June 1982
Major: Industrial Marketing
Honors: Dean's List

Queensborough Community College, New York
Degree: Associate in Applied Science in Data Processing

After

St. John's University, New York
MBA: Marketing Management, June 1984
3.4 G.P.A.

Bernard M. Baruch College, New York
BBA: Industrial Marketing, June 1982
Dean's List

Queensborough Community College, New York:
AS: Data Processing, June 1980

R U L E 2 4

For recent college graduates, education preceeds work experience.

FOR new job hunters, it is expected that "Educational Experience" will head up the résumé body copy. Unless you were an individual who worked full time before attending college, or unless you attended night school and were employed by day, you have limited work experience. What you *do* have to offer an employer is your newly earned degree and state-of-the-art training and technology in your field.

Every year, thousands of new graduates are absorbed into the labor force. The first ones hired are generally those with popular degrees; second are those candidates who are able to market themselves creatively to employers. This means that, despite the absence of a highly sought-after degree, the individual has positioned himself/herself in a desirable spot in the marketplace. One way to accomplish this is with a résumé that doesn't just sum up a limited past, but projects the individual's goals and expected contributions to the organization. Employers want candidates who look more like valuable employees than inexperienced graduates.

R U L E 2 5

Offer a selection of core courses only if they are relevant to the job objective.

IN general, candidates offer information on course concentration for the following reasons:

- to enable the employer to get a broader understanding of the course of study;
- to demonstrate proficiencies in special subject areas; and
- to fill out limited work experience when the candidate has had minimal exposure to the field relative to his/her career objective.

An individual who opts to include course concentration must never list a course by its number, or include the total credits earned for one or more courses in the area.

We advise most résumé writers to avoid the inclusion of courses. The truth is, most employers simply ignore this information. They are more interested in the school you attended and your degree than your program.

In the following résumé excerpt, the candidate did a fine job in the visual aspects of the design. However, we feel the information following "Studies include" for the three degrees listed is completely unnecessary. We would have preferred to see a connection made between the Environmental Studies and the Advanced Business degree. This individual could be a highly marketable commodity if he/she were to describe internships, part-time employment and special research. Résumé writers must take care not to include just *any* information, but the *right* information!

EDUCATION:

M.B.A. Finance (Marketing minor), May 1985
State University of New York at Albany, Albany, New York

Awarded Graduate Research Assistantship.

Studies include: • Competitive Strategies and Industry Analysis
• Credit Analysis
• Market Information Systems

M.A. Biology—Environmental Science, May 1982
Indiana University, Bloomington, Indiana

Awarded Graduate Teaching Assistantship.

Studies include: • Analytical and Organic Chemistry
• Environmental Law, Management, Restoration, and Impact Analysis

B.S. Biology—Environmental Science, cum laude, May 1980
Marist College, Poughkeepsie, New York

Awarded Presidential Scholarship.
Member Sigma Zeta Science Honor Society.

Studies include: • Chemistry • Mathematics • Energy Sciences
• Geology • Physics • Economics

R U L E 2 6

Never brag about a mediocre average.

THIS sounds like such a practical rule, yet so many résumé writers proceed to break it. We are amazed that job-seekers would even consider including poor averages (C or D grades) on their résumés. Your class rank or cumulative average *must* be impressive to warrant a mention on your résumé. This means that on a 4.0 scale (this figure is understood unless you indicate otherwise) you must possess at least a 3.3 average (B+).

Cumulative grades may be found on your final school transcript, or you may ask the registrar at your school to help you to accurately compute your grade point average. To note class rank as opposed to cumulative average, your ranking must be in the upper third of your class.

Keep mediocre grades away from the employer; but when you are a scholar, be sure to note it!

In the following example, the grade point average of this candidate was too low to be included. The figure should have been omitted.

EDUCATION

Bachelor of Science Degree in Business Administration
University of Vermont, Burlington, Vermont
Concentration in Finance and Human Resource Management
Graduated in May 1985   GPA 2.9

R U L E 2 7

Show off . . . if you graduated with honors or received special awards, say so!

HONORS and awards indicate ambition, motivation, and the ability to perform under pressure. Any awards you received as a graduate or undergraduate student should be included in the "Education" section of your résumé. As long as you don't become infatuated with any special recognition, and keep the inclusion of awards tasteful and conservative, employers will respond in a positive manner.

Items for consideration include:

Dean's List
Phi Betta Kappa
Summa Cum Laude
Magna Cum Laude
Cum Laude
Honor Roll
Special scholarships awarded by the University
Inclusion in publications such as *Who's Who in American Universities and Colleges*
Special academic awards for majors in your field

————— R U L E   2 8 —————

The most recent academic degree
should be listed first and proceed backward.
If the subject is a college graduate,
high school information is unnecessary.
Never include high school grades or test scores.

AN individual's education should be outlined as it was done with the work history, in inverse chronological order. Candidates are advised to begin with their most advanced or most recent educational experience, then work backward until they reach their bachelor's degree.

If a candidate is a college graduate, it is assumed that he/she is also a high school graduate; therefore, it is not necessary to list. We have been asked about the inclusion of a prestigious high school or preparatory school. This is a case where the inclusion may work for or against you. In some employment circles, the naming of a prestigious school may guarantee you immediate attention; however, you may also be labeled an academic snob. Therefore, it is our belief that any high school experience be omitted if one is a college graduate.

If you have not attended college, or did not graduate, be sure to include the highest level of education completed and an item regarding your high school diploma. Candidates who have earned partial credit toward an advanced degree should note this on their résumés. Vocational training may also be included.

Finally, regardless of how big a hero you may have been in high school or grade school, don't include this information on your résumé. Employers are not interested in your grades, final class standing, or your college entrance examination scores.

Do be careful to include accurate dates of attendance/ graduation, the school name and location, as well as the degree earned.

Poor Examples

This candidate obviously had exceptional scores on college entrance exams; however, it is inappropriate to include this information on a résumé at this level of education.

Education   Pelham Memorial High School, Pelham, NY
                   Graduated, June 1966

                   SAT: 791 math, 727 verbal
                   Achievement: 800 math, 735 physics,
                                658 chemistry
                   LSAT: 695

                   University of South Florida, Sarasota, FL
                   Graduated 1970, B.A. economics
                   Fordham Law School, N.Y., NY
                   1971-73

In the following examples, candidates made several errors: order of educational sequence is reversed; information has been omitted, e.g., school, location, degree, and/or course of study.

EDUCATION   **New Utrecht High School**
                   New York, N.Y.
                   Academic Diploma—1973

                   University of Miami
                   Miami, Fla.
                   B.A. Major: Marketing—1977

                           * * *

Education

George Wash. Univ.1968–71   B.A., Psychology
Catholic University 1976–77 Graduate Coursework in Social
                             Work
Georgetown Univ. 1981–82   Legal Assistant Program w/
                             Certificate

Education

1965–68:	Stranahan High School Fort Lauderdale, Fla.
1968–70:	University of Tennessee Knoxville, Tenn. (1½ years)
1971–72:	Katharine Gibbs Secretarial School Boston, Mass.

Good Examples

EDUCATION:
THE AMERICAN UNIVERSITY—Washington, DC
Washington College of Law, JD, 1973

BOSTON UNIVERSITY LAW SCHOOL, 1970–71

BOSTON UNIVERSITY—BA, 1970

BAR MEMBERSHIPS:
New York State, 1984; Washington, DC, 1973

* * *

EDUCATION

Seton Hall University, South Orange, NJ
    MBA in Marketing   currently attending
Columbia University, New York, NY
    MS in Engineering   1967
City College of New York, New York, NY
    BS in Engineering   1965

Additional courses in economics, management, communications, engineering, data processing; completed Bell Labs graduate study program.

PROFESSIONAL AFFILIATIONS

Women and Men in Telecommunications
Institute of Electrical and Electronics Engineers

RULE 29

List extracurricular activities, internships and part-time employment to display leadership traits and motivation.

IF you were an active participant in activities or employment relating to your major (career objective), you should note this involvement on your résumé. Employers appreciate well-rounded personalities; school activities can suggest a side other than your academic self.

If you had an interesting internship or worked part-time while attending school, you may include this information here or under "Employment." Candidates who financed their undergraduate or graduate degree may point this out on their résumés. Such a statement demonstrates the individual to be industrious with a healthy work ethic, for example: "Financed 100% of undergraduate tuition expenses through part-time employment and university scholarship."

School activities that directly apply to your career goals are the ones which should demand the most attention. If you held an office or were instrumental in a group's activities, include this information to indicate your capabilities to handle a demanding courseload and varied campus responsibilities. If the activity was not with an easily recognizable group, a word or two of explanation may be appropriate. Be wary of including a long list of activities, particularly those which convey a lack of seriousness. Employers may wonder when you had time to study amid your popularity or they may consider you to be more of a "party-goer" than a "team player."

Examples

ACHIEVEMENTS AND ACTIVITIES (SUNY Cortland):
★ N.Y.S. Chancellor's Excellence in Teaching Awards Nominations
   Committee
★ Rape Prevention Adhoc Committee—Organizer
★ Off-Campus Student's Social Organization—Founder/President
★ Intercollegiate Debate Team—Captain
   Dormitory Social Functions Committee—Chairperson
   Dormitory Home Coming Float Committee—Chairperson
   Campus Dorm Repairs Investigations Adhoc Committee—Co-
   Chairperson
★ Student Body Senator
   Universities Ice Arena Advisory Board
   Campus Newspaper Photographer
   Political Science Club
   Cortland State Rugby Club

   (High School)
   Senior and Freshman Class President

This student was extremely active but the list was too long, so we made suggestions as to which activities should be included. They are starred.

Extracurricular Activities and Honors:	American Marketing Association
	University Marketing Club and Committees
	University Finance Society
	University 1983 Towers Council Representative
	Hartford County 4-H offices and awards
	Hartford Courant Creative Writing Award

This student appears active and yet focused, with an obvious interest in Marketing. This interest was complemented by participation in related activities—finance and creative writing.

RULE 30

Include continuing education courses and professional seminars.

INDIVIDUALS with solid work experience must indicate their willingness to keep up with today's technology and modern business philosophy. By participating in continuing education courses or professional seminars, the candidate displays an ongoing quest for education. Employers approve of the ability to learn and incorporate new techniques into practical work experiences. If you have attended any professional development programs, list them on your résumé; it is not necessary to indicate whether they were self-paid or company-sponsored.

Examples

PROFESSIONAL DEVELOPMENT

General Electric Company: Technical Marketing Program, Management Development Course, Modern Marketing Course, Advanced Management Seminar

EDUCATION

Graduate   **New York University**
(1981-1984)   100 Washington Square East, New York

Advanced Playwriting
Writing for Film & Television

New York School for Social Research
66 West 12th Street, New York

Advanced Screenwriting
Intensive Filmmaking Workshop
*Advanced Video Production Workshop
Development & Packaging of T.V. & Cable

Undergraduate   **Brooklyn College (CUNY)**
Bachelor of Arts—English, June 1979
cum laude

*Received certificate

CONTINUING   *General Electric Training Programs*
EDUCATION: • Report Writing School
• Kepner Tregoe Decision Making Course
• First Line Supervisors Workshop
• Personal Computers School (Lotus 1-2-3)
• New Communicators Clinic

* * *

N.Y.S. Certified in Care of the Mentally and Physically Handicapped. Includes specific certification in:
— Medication. Took 40-hour course which required demonstrated
ability to prepare client and administer prescriptions.
— Basic First Aid Practices. 20-hour Red Cross course encompass-
ing bandaging, resuscitation and emergency treatment of cuts
and burns.

R U L E 3 1

Never include the names, titles or phone numbers of references.

IT is completely unprofessional to supply the names of your references on your résumé. It may be extremely bothersome to the named individuals, and one of the most common errors made by résumé-writers everywhere. Only indicate that you do indeed have references. The customary phrase is, "References Furnished (or Available) Upon Request." Be prepared to have two employment-related references and one personal reference.

Some candidates attempt to impress a reader by listing the names of affluent or well-known individuals—when it comes to references, it will not matter who you know, but rather what they say about you.

Examples

REFERENCES FURNISHED UPON REQUEST
A portfolio will be furnished upon request. Excellent personal and professional references will be furnished when a mutual interest has been established.

* * *

REFERENCES
Available on request from Career Development Center, Union College, Schenectady, New York 12308 (518) 555-0000.

RULE 32

Ask an individual for his/her permission before releasing a name as a reference. Make sure your reference has a copy of your résumé.

EMPLOYERS *do* check references.

When you select your references, choose people who know you well and who are able to speak candidly and positively about your work habits and strengths.

There are a few additional rules to keep in mind when it comes to references.

- Be sure you have on hand a current listing of your reference's phone number, title, and place of employment. It can be embarrassing and/or awkward to offer an old phone number or inaccurate information, making you appear unorganized and showing that you are out of touch with this person who supposedly knows you well enough to comment on your abilities.

- Be courteous and call to obtain the permission of an individual, allowing you to use this person as a reference. Don't let the employer surprise him/her by calling first.

- Forward a copy of your résumé to your references. This can be helpful in several ways: as a memory refresher, as a base of information for a reference to expand on when called, and as a networking tool for references who may be able to pass your résumé onto appropriate colleagues.

- If you have married or had a name change, be sure to alert your references of this change. It would be awful for an employer to do a reference check and have the reference respond that they do not know anyone by that name.
- When you accept a position, write a short thank-you note to let your reference(s) know you appreciated his/her help. This is not only good etiquette, but smart business. References are important, professional contacts and you never know when you may need to call on them again.

R U L E   3 3

Review your résumé.
Information that must be omitted includes: birthdate, marital status, interests/hobbies, health status, height/weight, religious affiliation, political beliefs, photograph and any other extemporaneous information.

WE have seen résumés that included the most incredible personal information... dress size, monthly rent, children's birthdates. Yes, we are serious!

Here is the rule: DO NOT INCLUDE PERSONAL INFORMATION! That's it. Simple and direct. Ignore what you have heard or read, employers simply do not care about most of the information supplied under "Personal."

Many job-hunters list that they are married to show stability. However, a woman who lists her marital status may be setting herself up for elimination from consideration. While it is illegal for employers to ask certain personal questions, if you offer the information on your own, you have no recourse. A married woman may be eliminated because the employer fears she will leave to have children, or she will not be able to put in the necessary overtime. It is unfair, but it happens. Be smart — keep confidential information off your résumé.

Equal employment laws have made it illegal for employers to ask you your age, and we may add... age is becoming less and less of an issue. Do not include your date of birth, social security number or health status. (Everyone *always* writes "excellent.")

Photographs are frowned on and project an old-fashioned, unsophisticated image. Interests and hobbies may give your reader a chuckle — while you may love a particular hobby, the employer may find it silly.

When we've questioned a candidate as to why he/she included certain information, the response has been that they wanted the employer to see them as a person. Let us remind you that the employer is looking for an employee, not a friend. What is important is that you can do the job and do it well.

If you prepare an effective résumé you will get the interview. Wait for the interview to work on "chemistry." A face-to-face discussion is truly a much better way to get to know someone than by reading about his/her interests on paper. We understand that personal interests and certain facts are important to you but have no place on your résumé.

The following are actual excerpts from résumés we have received!

PERSONAL
Married with two children. Excellent health.

* * *

AUTHOR of 39 books and pamphlets (poetry and new arts criticism). MARRIED; twin daughters aged 20; enjoy nature, music, cooking. Speak GERMAN (fluent), FRENCH; read LATIN, SWEDISH.

* * *

Working experience began at 9...very interested in the field of marketing...enjoy jogging, reading and Kung Fu. Willing to travel.

* * *

PERSONAL   Marital Status: Single
DATA: Date of Birth: May 13, 1943
                 Two independent children
                 Health: Excellent
                 I am ambitious, and enjoy learning new things
                 that is why as you can see by my experience I
                 never take the same type of job twice. I need to
                 learn and grow.

* * *

PERSONAL INTERESTS
God, church, fellowship. Christian art. Guitar and piano. Travel. Painting.

PERSONAL INFORMATION:

Date of Birth: October 9, 1955   Height: 5'9"
Place of Birth: Smyrna, Tenn.   Weight: 155 lbs.
Marital Status: Married   Social Sec. #: 000-000-0000
Health: Excellent   Driver's License: Yes

INTERESTS: Photography (I'm good); writing essays, short stories and bad poems (usually aboard planes or on Staten Island ferry); family camping; collecting rocks, minerals, seashells and rejection slips (have been published in consumer travel magazine); extensive reading; most participation sports; lots of non-business travel.

* * *

Personal

Single...5'9"...135lbs...health excellent...enjoy music, theater, swimming and fitness...believe that honesty and commitment to service are keys to success.

* * *

Personal: Age 45, Devout Irish-American Roman Catholic (Nine First Fridays—27 times, no meat on Friday, daily stations of the Cross, Mass in Latin only)

Married (Absolutly no birth control activities of any kind.) 4 children

───── R U L E 3 4 ─────

Do not include an introduction
or concluding statement
as to why the employer should hire you.

THE résumé must be free of information that does not
contribute to the candidate's specific qualifications for employment. Every word, every sentence must focus on getting you the
interview. Unfortunately, some résumé writers carry this thinking a bit too far. Many writers get "sloppy" and spoil a great
résumé by adding a tagline of unnecessary information. A cover
letter is a much more appropriate place to sum up your skills
and talents. Do not feel that you must make a personal statement
about yourself just in case the employer remains unconvinced of
your talents. These "summaries" rarely clinch the interview.
More often than not, they cast the vote in the other direction.

Do *not* follow the excerpt examples below.

INTRODUCING: A RENAISSANCE MAN...FOR RENT

* * *

STATEMENT   My proven managerial/supervisory skills, along
with the ability to organize and meet deadlines
should prove advantageous to a future employer.
Customer service/relations, communication
skills and a talent for flexibility have featured
prominently in my positions.

SUMMARY   Experience and aptitude to be an asset to an organization seeking an individual who is knowledgeable in sales and marketing. Goal oriented and willing to give 150% to a position where increased responsibilities will lead to company and personal growth. Have both education and practical experience in management which can be applied to a variety of situations. Take pride in personal appearance and the ability to deal with others in professional situations.

* * *

THANK YOU, for your consideration. I'd like to arrange an interview regarding the position you have, or may make available. You may contact me at my residence at your convenience if you have any questions or would like to set up an appointment.

RULE 35

Use appropriate main headings in the format of the résumé.

As you review your résumé, notice how you have pulled together specific information. Your headings should act as a guide or lead-in for the information that follows in the body copy.

The headings catch the reader's eye first and therefore must not only be worded appropriately, but must be visually compelling. Your headings must establish a communication link with your readers and target in on both your experiences and goals. We've prepared a list of headings that are suitable for résumé use.

Career Objective/Goal	Education
Employment Experience	Professional Education
Work History	Certificates and Licenses
Business Experience	Special Skills
Professional Highlights	Special Projects
Selected Achievements	Technical Skills
Selected Accomplishments	Citations and Awards
Relevant Experience	Publications
Business Affiliations	Military Experience
Memberships	Languages
Organizations	References

Be conservative rather than gimmicky. We recently received on résumé with these not-so-clever titles: *Proposed Contribution*, *Qualifications Summary*, *Indicators of Capability*, *Comments*, and *Other Facts*.

R U L E 3 6

Include military experience only if it explains a gap in work history or education.

MILITARY experience is only necessary if it explains a time lapse in your work history. If service experience has no relevance to your intended career, simply state that you completed your service and were honorably discharged. It is acceptable to include the branch of service, dates, and rank. If you learned special skills while in the military that add to your employment qualifications, be sure to highlight them.

Example

MILITARY   U.S. Army, 1967–1971
Staff Sergeant, Corps of Engineers
Received training in drafting of bridges and roads.
Honorably discharged.

R U L E   3 7

Special skills may be included,
but be selective.

"SPECIAL Skills" offer the candidate the opportunity to include those abilities that might otherwise have gone unnoticed. Skills can be transferred to various situations and make the candidate a well-rounded, versatile human being.

Technical skills are tangible skills involving some degree of special training. The individual has learned something specific that may be presented in concrete, rather than abstract, terms. These include: computer or word processing training, typing, fluency in a foreign language(s), photography, public speaking, and specialized writing skills, to name just a few.

Soft or *functional* skills are those skills not easily defined or exhibited. They do, however, contribute to the overall make-up of the candidate, for example: planning, organizing, and the ability to interact with others (human relations).

If you opt to include an area on your résumé titled, "Special Skills," think carefully about what information will be included. Save "soft" skills for your cover letter; incorporate these talents into your pitch for employment. Be sure that those technical skills listed on your résumé augment your employment qualifications and add to your marketability.

Examples

TECHNICAL SKILLS

Operate: Studio cameras, porta paks, character generator, "3/4" panasonic convergence editing system, "3/4" Sony U-matic professional editing system, Panasonic "1/2" editing system, light kits, etc.

* * *

SPECIAL SKILLS

Typing 70 words per minute. Dictaphone 55 words per minute. Experienced with IBM Mainframe 3033, IBM PC, Apple II, Digital Rainbow.

RULE 38

Save artwork and/or writing skills for your portfolio.

Do not include artwork or writing samples with your résumé. Individuals in fields where these special art forms are valued, should spend considerable time and energy building a quality portfolio consisting of samples of their work. This portfolio should be reviewed with the employer at the time of the interview.

Your résumé should not contain any of your original work, but should serve as a listing of your credentials, for example:

- Where have you been published?
- What advertising campaigns have you created?
- Where have you exhibited your art?
- Have you done free-lance assignments? If so, for whom?

We've included an excerpt from the résumé of a commercial artist. The candidate nicely encapsulates skills and indicates a portfolio is available for viewing.

Graphic artist with 5 years experience. Skilled in illustration, design, layout, paste-up, lettering, color separation, type spec, comps, and film-stripping. Work experience has primarily been with small ad agencies and free-lance. General range of subjects and applications include:

- Pencil illustrations
- Pen and ink
- Full color
- Magazine and newspaper ads
- Designs
- Storyboards
- Signs and posters

- Brochures
- Technical illustrations
- Drafting
- Decorative painting
- T-shirt art
- Logo design
- Paste-up for printers

Portfolio and references available upon request.

R U L E   3 9

No borders or artwork on a résumé.
Graphic designers/artists
have limited freedom here,
but any design should be
conservative, small, and tasteful.

CANDIDATES should never submit a résumé outlined with a border or any additional artwork — with one exception. The rare exception is someone employed or seeking employment within the graphic arts industry. In such a case, the résumé often serves as a medium to convey a small, yet tasteful sampling of the subject's work.

We want to make a point of stating that we receive a great many résumés from individuals anxiously seeking employment as artists, graphic designers, and illustrators. Surprisingly enough, many of these same candidates do not appear to give their résumés any thought in terms of visual appeal, which is ridiculous considering their job objective. We suggest that you treat your résumé as you would a piece of your best work. The typeface should be clean and attractive, the layout nicely thought out, and the overall appearance should be eye-catching.

R U L E 4 0

Review the résumé's style and tone.
Keep it objective: avoid narrative descriptions
and the use of *I*, *me*, *my*, etc.

DON'T let your résumé read like a letter or short story. *Résumé* is from a French word meaning *summary*. Therefore, your headings and text must be concise and to the point.

Formal sentence structure takes up space and is unnecessary. Since the subject is *you*, the use of *I* is understood, rather than written. Implied pronouns save valuable space and help avoid the impression of boastfulness or egotism. Employers want to read brisk, businesslike statements; the more successful you are in conveying such an image, the greater your chances of success in securing an interview.

Poor Examples

The following is a clear-cut case of the "I's Have it!" The subject comes off like an unappealing braggart.

Miscellaneous —English, German and French are languages in which I am fluent.
—I am member of the Association of the MBA executives.
—I am a Staff member of the Investment club of the Institute of Affairs.
—In the Rugby team of Metz, I was third line.
—I also take part in horse riding competitions.
—I like to travel and have been to most European countries.
—I have lived in Algeria, South Africa and the United States.

This next writer is telling a story not writing a résumé with information that is unnecessary and inappropriate.

MY POLICY WITH EMPLOYEES HAS ALWAYS BEEN A SIMPLE ONE, THAT PEOPLE PERFORM BETTER IF THEY ENJOY WHAT THEY ARE DOING, AND THROUGH SCHEDULING AND OC-CASIONAL RETRAINING, I HAVE ALWAYS MADE EVERY EF-FORT TO MAINTAIN A PLEASANT WORK ENVIRONMENT.

THE UPCOMING SALE OF OUR COMPANY AFFORDS ME THE OPPORTUNITY TO FINALLY PURSUE A CAREER IN THE ENTERTAINMENT INDUSTRY, WITH WHICH I HAVE ALWAYS BEEN CONNECTED ON A PART-TIME BASIS.

Employment

I do not like writing résumés. I prefer interviews, face-to-face discussions. Therefore, there will be no long list of names and addresses of former employers, except as noted below. Further information and references can be furnished upon request.

What an opening line! A typical employer's response might be, "And I dislike reading résumés!" No employer will attempt to contact you if you fail to produce a preview of those qualifications making you an attractive candidate.

R U L E   4 1

Never attempt to be cute or gimmicky.

"CUTE" rarely works.

Of course, there is a rather famous, if dubious story of an advertising hopeful who wanted to break into one of the Top 10 ad agencies. A traditional résumé was tried, but competition was stiff. After pondering the problem for some time, the idea of printing the résumé on a T-shirt and packaging it in a crisp Brooks Brothers box complete with tissue paper and ribbon was arrived at. This "creation" was sent off to a well-known creative director at a 4A agency. The director loved the originality and the candidate was hired, later becoming a successful assistant creative director with the firm.

Now for the bad news... that's a Cinderella story and it may or may not be true. We suspect that if it actually did happen, the chances of similar success are limited.

A survey of a wide representation of personnel people from diverse fields turned up a group consensus that recruiters prefer traditional, conservative résumés — and, we have to agree.

Our mail is occasionally laced with résumés in the forms of brochures, or greeting cards, or sheet music; once we even received a telegram. The impression of the subject is that the candidate is slightly crazy, unprofessional and perhaps even a bit desperate. Our advice, especially to that stoic group of non-conformists, is to keep your résumé low-key and businesslike. Refrain from allowing zany or gimmicky statements to creep into your text. Read our real-life excerpts that follow and decide if you would have invited the candidate in for an interview.

But you don't want to read a lot of past history—
   You want to talk to me about my present and our future!

* * *

I want to work with an intelligent, obstinate, accurate, sensitive
   human being who happens to direct a department of
   precisely the same sort of people.
Are you that ever-elusive being?
Then I'm interested in you.

* * *

   My goals are easy to relate. I'd like to spend my
declining years (30 on, I guess) writing best-selling
novels and Pulitizer Prize-winning plays. In the meantime
I want to work with pleasant, creative people in a position
where I can use my head and pen to the advantage of all
concerned. I expect to be paid a fair wage for which I will
assume all the responsibility (and more) inherent with the
job. I'm a very nice person despite what my landlady says.
I just happen to like The Moody Blues played above a
whisper. So sue me!

R U L E 4 2

A résumé must be visually inviting.

SOMEONE once told us that a résumé has to fall into the category of "Get It... Got It... Good!" What does this mean? First, it means that visual appeal gets the reader's attention... straightforward text grabs the reader's interest... and the overall impression is "Good... I want this person at my organization!"

For many résumé-writers, layout is a major pitfall. It does not take an artistic eye to make a page attractive or readable, it takes common sense. Your résumé is the first contact the employer has with you. A résumé that is hard to read or confusing will be tossed immediately. Your résumé's physical appearance is every bit as important as the text itself.

An attractive résumé will be given extra consideration and the employer will want to find out more about the candidate.

Average credentials displayed attractively will get more attention than outstanding credentials displayed poorly.

R U L E   4 3

Utilize margins correctly;
do not allow your résumé to be
top/bottom heavy or lopsided.

ON a résumé, the white space is called the "ground." Use it effectively so the reader is not overwhelmed with information. A résumé must be centered with ample margins on all sides of the text. There should be 1 to 1½ inches of white space at the top and bottom of the page and at least 1 inch of white on the left- and right-hand side of the paper. Keep your right margin consistent, do not let your text stray to the edge of the paper.

Beware of the top- or bottom-heavy résumé. This occurs when the text is incorrectly distributed. Do not have too much or too little body copy in either area. Take the paper-fold test: Fold your résumé in half lengthwise and then in half by width. Reopen your paper. You should have four quadrants as defined by the creases. Imagine these folds to be dividing lines. The text should be balanced on both sides of the lines, as though reading a mirror image.

The following illustrates, with *before* and *after* excerpts what we mean.

Before

Education

St. John's University, Jamaica, New York
67 credits toward B.A. in Finance

Queensborough College, Bayside, New York
Associates Degree in Accounting (6/80)

Hardware

Wang PC, Hyperion, Compaq, IBM PC, VM/CMS

Software

dBase II, Multiplan, Lotus 1-2-3

After

Education	St. John's University, Jamaica, NY 67 credits earned toward a B.A. in Finance Queensborough College, Bayside, NY A.S. in Accounting 1980
Hardware	Wang PC, Hyperion, Compaq, IBM PC, VM/CMS
Software	dBase II, Multiplan, Lotus 1-2-3

Before

Professional Objective

To obtain a position of responsibility with a business or agency in the area of administration and personnel.

Education

University of Maryland, Eastern Shore (UMES)
Princess Anne, Maryland 21853

Recipient of B.S. degree in May 1981.
Majored in business administration management and a minor in economics.

Financed expenses by part-time work, grants and partial university scholarship.

After

Professional Objective:

To obtain a position of responsibility with a business or agency in the area of administration and personnel.

Education:
May 1981

University of Maryland, Princess Anne, MD
B.S. in Business Administration
Economics Minor

Financed expenses by part-time work, grants and partial university scholarship.

R U L E   4 4

If the résumé is professionally typeset, make careful use of boldface, italics, and underscores.

WE firmly believe a professionally typeset résumé makes a dramatic impact on the reader.

You can recognize professionally set type as opposed to typewriter type. The typeset material looks classier...elegant...finished. Typeset material is proportionally spaced. This means words are put together according to the width of the letters that they are composed of. A typed word devotes the same amount of space to each letter. For example, a typed *i* gets the same amount of space as a *w* even though the *i* is narrower. In proportional type, an adjustment is made for the varying width of letters. This book is typeset.

If you have your résumé professionally typeset, you should ask the compositor for advice regarding layout and lettering. Choose an attractive typeface, and make use of boldface lettering, italics, and/or underscores. The following presents excerpts from professionally typeset résumés.

Associate Director of Trade Manufacturing

Supervise a four-person department, which takes 150 titles a year from manuscript through bound book. Totally familiar with web and sheet fed offset printing, single through multicolor process. Fully versed in computer composition and diskette conversions.

GREATER PHILADELPHIA CHAMBER OF COMMERCE   12/84–8/85
Assistant Manager Technology Council   5/85–8/85

- Managed publication and distribution of *Technology Council News* (printing, layout, mailing, etc.)
- Interviewed corporate executives, institute directors, and research managers
- Wrote *Technology Council News* (circulation—2000)
- Researched market for special seminar for Institutional Investors
- Edited PACE program newsletter—(Philadelphia Area Council for Excellence)

* * *

EDUCATION

State University College at New Paltz, New Paltz, NY
Professional Certification in Administration   **1977**

State University College at Oneonta, Oneonta, NY
M.S. Degree in Education   **1974**

State University College at Plattsburgh, Plattsburgh, NY
B.S. Degree in Education   **1965**

Additional Coursework in Public Relations, Negotiation, Communications and Group Analytical Planning.

R U L E   4 5

If your résumé is typed, be fussy.
Letters should be crisp and clean.
Use a readable element in
uppercase and lowercase letters.

IF you can't afford to have your résumé professionally typeset, a typed version will suffice. The key word is *quality*. The characters/letters must be crisp and clean. There must be no broken capitals or ribbon smudges. If possible, take your résumé to someone who can type it on a high-quality office machine. The faithful portable that saw you through college and beyond will not do. If the typist has access to various type elements or daisy wheels, ask to see what the different typefaces look like, and choose a type that suits you and your business interests.

- Never prepare a résumé in a script typeface. It will appear flowery and unprofessional.
- Never type your résumé in all uppercase letters, it will be too difficult to read.
- Check for broken letters, smudged punctuation marks, and closed letters.

The following are samples of typed résumés—do *not* use them as role models!

Manager, Personnel Operations--ALSA International
Have been responsible for the administration of all
policies and procedures including recruiting, labor
relations, benefits, contractss, compensation, payroll,
records, training, orientation, facilities, recreation,
project, staffing forecasts and labor regulation
compliance as well as general and eemployee
information serrvices for an organization of 200
employees.

SKILLS :
RECEPTIONIST
SWITCHBOARD OPER.
FILING
XEROXING
MAIL CLERK
METER MAIL (COMPUTER)
LOGGING (RECORD KEEPING)
COMPUTER CASHIER
40WPM-TYPING

Employment Responsibilities-- *The everyday repairs and*
upkeep of one of the school buildings in the district; maintenance
and repairs on the electrical, heating, and plumbing systems;
some carpentry and cabinet making; other minor improvements
that did not qualify for outside contractual bidding.

6/80 - 8/84   **DEKALB COUNTY POLICE DEPT.-DECATUR, GA
POLICE DETECTIVE -UNDERCOVER NARCOTICS
INVESTIGATIONS - LEAD UNIT 3 CONSECUTIVE
MONTHS IN NARCOTIC RELATED BUYS AND
ARRESTS. ALSO GENERAL THEFT INVESTIGATION
OF THEFT VIOLATIONS EXCLUDING BURGLARY
AND ROBBERY - AVERAGE CLEARANCE RATE 8 8 %.
PATROL OFFICER-TRAFFIC CONTROL, CRIME
PREVENTION AND INVESTIGATION. KEEP ORDER,
ASSIST PUBLIC.**

R U L E   4 6

Be consistent throughout
in the use of format.

IF you decide to have your section headings typed or typeset in capital letters, all of the headings must follow the same format. If you underscore your job title, each and every job title within your various employment experiences should also be underscored.

Keep your margins consistent, neat and aligned. Be consistent with the use of boldface, punctuation, italics, underscored words, and type size.

RULE 47

An individual should be able to tell his/her story on a résumé that is one page in length; two-page maximum for senior executives.

THE ideal résumé is one page in length. The text should fill out the page in readable type with appropriate margins. If you feel you have to omit critical information by limiting yourself to one page, then go with the two-page format—but stop there! Every item should be of key importance—no wasted words.

Employers will tell you that a short résumé is preferable to one that goes on for pages (and many of them do). Employers may judge your ability to set priorities, as well as the ability to get to the facts by noting what you chose to include on your résumé. Too often résumé-writers keep going because they feel they must get every last detail down on paper.

Give your reader pertinent data filled with relevant experiences. Employers should not have to wade through verbiage in an effort to find something that strikes them as interesting.

If you have your résumé typeset, the usual rule to follow is 1½ pages of typewriter type equals 1 page of typeset type. Be a discriminating editor, always look for phrases that can be worded more succinctly and/or delete redundant information.

R U L E   4 8

A résumé should conform to
one's level of employment
in terms of layout, paper quality,
and appearance of body copy.

THIS rule simply means that if you are an executive commanding a $50,000 a year salary, then you shouldn't skimp on your résumé. It should measure up to your own expectations for yourself. Senior executives should have their résumés typeset and reproduced on high-quality linen paper stock. No quick or tacky reproductions on the office copier.

College graduates are expected to have nicely typed résumés, but mid-level executives should try for as polished an image as possible. That means typeset or word processed text.

How your résumé appears to the reader at the onset, conveys your professional identity, and sets the tone for what the employer imagines you to be like.

RULE 49

Proofread it!
Absolutely no typographical errors,
misspelled words or grammatical mistakes.

YOU'VE heard this one before...carefully proof your copy. Correct any errors before you go through the trouble and expense of reproducing your résumé. Once you have examined it thoroughly for errors and typos, ask two friends to check it again for you. We have heard of candidates who have had great success by proofreading their résumés by reading the text backwards, line by line. When you read a page in the normal way you may subconsciously correct an obvious error; you understand the content so you don't notice the mistake. This is much harder to do when you are reading in reverse.

Somehow employers almost always catch the typos on the first run through. "When I find a résumé with an error I automatically eliminate the candidate," a personnel director for a large hospital told us. "There is absolutely no reason that this error should have gotten by the writer or anyone else who carefully proofed it. An error to me signifies a lack of care and implies that the candidate will make the same sort of mistake if I hire him or her for my organization."

Employers love perfectionists! Pay attention to details! Can you find the errors in the following excerpts?

1.

August 1979–
May 1980
Washington Memorial Hospital, Washington, DC
Senior File Clerk
Functioned as backup receptionist; set up transportation for arae out-patience; maintained extensive hospital records; light typing and xeroxing.

2.

Personnel Assistant
Hamburger Press, Inc. Iowa City, Iowa
- Exposure to EEO policies and proceedures
- Process paperwork for worker's compensation cases
- Screen and interview job candidates for various department
- Coordinate employer attendance records and weekly payroll

3.

REFRENCES: Furnished upon request

Answers:
1. arae — area
    patience — patients

2. proceedures — procedures
    department — departments
    employer — employee

3. REFRENCES — REFERENCES

RULE 50

Never underline a point by hand for emphasis.
Do not write on a printed résumé
(this includes corrections or amendments).

WHEN something as formal as a résumé is in its final state, don't ruin an excellent job by making corrections by hand. We have seen exceptional-looking résumés completely spoiled by the use of heavy underlining by a wide felt-tip marking pen to indicate a point of possible interest to the reader. Such marks are distracting and unattractive.

If your address has changed, white out the information on your original and have it typed in. Even a typed lable is neater than using a pen to write over printed information. The ideal solution, of course, is to have your résumé redone.

Don't do the following!

General Management	Reduced turnover and expenses of a 37-member department. Turnover down 35%, expenses 15%.
Marketing Planning	Increased sales from $2 to $6 in one year by territory realignment, design and institution of a compensation plan and direct target mailings.

R U L E   5 1

Have your résumé professionally reproduced.

MOST résumés should be updated every six months, so don't print a large quantity. They may become outdated quicker than your supply can be depleted.

For quantities of more than 100, but less than 1,000 have a professional printer Itek your résumé. You can locate a source for this by checking your local Yellow Page Directory and calling to compare the prices of various printers. Itek printing is an economical choice for anyone who wants a quantity of résumés reproduced. A paper plate is created and the final product is exceptionally clear. For more than 1,000 use Offset printing (a photo plate). *Hint:* ask your printer which is more cost effective—for you to supply your own paper stock or to have the printer include it in his cost.

The least expensive method for reproducing your résumé is to have it photocopied ("xeroxed"). Your neighborhood probably has several quick-copy shops where you can bring in a camera-ready copy of your résumé and have it copied while you wait. *Hint:* always ask to see a proof before the printer runs off your entire order, or a first copy from the copyperson. Photocopy machines are notorious for printing small black specks and/or smudges around the edges of the paper. These imperfections are generally easy to correct if you catch them at the start of the order.

One *don't*...never use your dot matrix printer from your home or personal computer to print your résumé. The results are very unprofessional.

RULE 52

A résumé should be printed on
high-quality paper stock.

IF you've ever held a piece of really fine paper in your hand, you know that texture and appearance can be extremely important. Examine the quality of paper your résumé is printed on...how does it stand up?

Résumé-writers should shop around for paper stock and become familiar with the assortment of papers available. We suggest that a résumé be printed on bond paper with a cotton rag content. This is slightly heavier than regular typing paper. Ask your stationer for a 20- to 24-pound stock with 25% cotton content bond. Paper taboos include onionskin, erasable bond and any continuous green bar or plain computer paper. *Hint:* buy blank matching stock and envelopes for use in mailing out your résumés and enclosing a matching cover letter.

R U L E 5 3

Résumés are best suited to colors such as cream, white, buff, or pale grey.

JOB candidates frequently think that if they choose an interesting paper color, their résumés will be more attractive. The fact is that colored stock makes you stand out from the crowd... like a sore thumb! If your résumé is on any shade of paper but the ones listed here, consider having it done over. We veto pinks, yellows, pale greens, pastel blues, and tans. Regardless of your choice of paper color, your ink color should always be black. Résumés that are printed on colored backgrounds are difficult to reproduce on any office copier. Thus, if an employer wants to pass a copy of your résumé onto a coworker, his attempt may be hampered by your poor choice of paper color.

RULE 54

A résumé should be 8½ × 11 in size.

ODD-SIZED paper may be visually attractive, but it can create a definite filing problem. Only 8½ × 11 paper should be used for a résumé. We met one eager candidate who was so intent on following the one-page-only rule that paper 8½ × 14 was used. This is a "Catch-22" situation that solves one problem but creates another. If you have a two-page résumé, each page should contain your name; the two pages should be stapled in the upper left-hand corner of the page. It is better to use two pieces of the 8½ × 11 paper than to try to cram your information onto one long page.

RULE 55

Print on one side of the page only; type size should be completely legible.

CANDIDATES try to circumvent the one-page rule by printing on both sides of the paper or by reducing the size of the type. This is a most unprofessional decision. Small type is difficult to read, as is something which has large blocks of print on both sides of the paper. Instead, edit or rewrite your text (to reduce volume) rather than try to solve the dilemma with an awkward solution.

Foreigners looking for employment in the U.S. should follow American business format in writing a résumé.

EVERY week, we receive at least 10 to 15 résumés from job candidates from foreign countries. These individuals are seeking employment in the United States, but have not adhered to our accepted résumé format. In order to be considered for employment, one has to play by the host's rules. Employers react negatively when they encounter something they are unfamiliar with or do not understand. Such would be the case of a résumé from a European or Far Eastern applicant.

Foreigners wishing employment in the United States must study our résumé format and modify their versions to our American tastes.

The following is an excerpt from a résumé of a British candidate. The education experience reads very differently from our format. This job-hunter needs to do some homework.

Education & Qualifications
PLACE
Austin Friars School_Carlisle.
Sept/67_June/72

Carlisle Tech. College.

Higher Education.

Trent Polytechnic_Nottingham.
(Sept/79_July/82)
Nottingham Univ. Oral exam.
(1985).

EXAMS PASSED
"O" Level _ English Literature.
_ Maths
_ Geography
_ Brit. Politics
"A" Level _ Soc & Economic Hist.
_ English Literature.

B.A. (Hons.) Social Sciences.

Credit.

R U L E 5 7

Always include a cover letter with your résumé when mailing it to prospective employers.

Do not sabotage your job-hunting efforts by mailing out a résumé without a cover letter, or worse, a hastily written one. Employers use a cover letter as a screening tool and they like to get a "personal" feel for the candidate through the letter. A well-written letter can neutralize the tone of the impersonal résumé and place you on "human terms" with the prospective employer. Furthermore, a cover letter allows the résumé-writer to tailor his/her interests to a particular opening—this is virtually impossible and impractical to do with a résumé.

A good cover letter addresses the following points:

- The reason for the letter. Is the individual responding to an ad, inquiring about current openings, or writing at the suggestion of a mutual contact?
- It explains why the writer is interested in employment at this firm. Does the candidate's experience coincide with the company's needs?
- It highlights major career accomplishments and refers the reader to the résumé for further details.
- It enables the candidate to request an interview.

Sample Cover Letter

Box 000
230 Park Avenue
New York, New York 10169

Dear Sir:

I read your ad for a "Marketing Director" in the April 23 edition of *The New York Times* with great interest.

My career includes six years in a variety of marketing and sales environments and I feel I can make significant contributions to your organization as you begin your national franchising program. Last year our sales revenues at my present employer increased by a rate of 48% and I am proud to say I was instrumental in obtaining these results. Through my efforts, we increased our direct mail distribution and began to penetrate the overseas market.

I have a full understanding of advertising theory, production and am able to negotiate and oversee relationships with outside vendors such as premium distributors, ad agencies and printers. I hold an MBA in Marketing from Ohio University and my undergraduate degree is in Business Administration.

I hope that we may set up a time where we can discuss how we can benefit each other. I will be calling you later this week to follow up. Thank you for your time and consideration. I am eager to put my talents to work for your organization.

Sincerely,

R U L E 5 8

Do not enclose your résumé
in a report cover or bulky package.
Never attach school transcripts or
letters of recommendation.

WE speak from experience when we say that no employer wants to receive a résumé enclosed in a plastic report cover or other material. A résumé is a stand-alone item, it should not be encumbered with school transcripts, letters from previous employers, or photocopies of awards.

The résumé has to do the job on its own. You will distract the reader and reduce the effectiveness of your résumé if you add additional documents to it. Let your résumé go "solo."

R U L E 5 9

Create several versions
of your résumé
with varied themes.

CANDIDATES rarely consider that they can have more than one résumé. If you have an interest in multiple areas, advertising and personnel for example, why not create two résumés where your experiences and skills are slanted toward these varying objectives? This is a perfectly permissible option and shows that you are a far-thinking, creative individual who is not about to be restricted by the boundaries and depth of one piece of paper.

We agree that it is hard enough to write one résumé; however, if you are motivated and want to keep as many career doors open as possible, you will consider this option.

RULE 60

Write your résumé yourself.

WHY? Because no one knows the subject better than you. Be patient, and willing to give the task time and thought. Eventually you will come up with a product to be proud of.

Employers will use your résumé as a reference point during the interview. By expressing your work history and skills in your own words, you will be able to flow smoothly from one topic to the next as it appears on your résumé.

Finally, there is a certain satisfaction that one feels after seeing the labor of writing a résumé go from idea to print. It is even more gratifying to be invited for an interview from a résumé that has been written and designed by you.

Look over your existing résumé. Was it prepared by you or by a professional résumé-writing service? Are you comfortable with the phrasing and vocabulary? Does the résumé say everything you would say about yourself if you were given the opportunity? This *is* your opportunity!

RÉSUMÉ:
—— BEFORE & AFTER ——

THE following *before* and *after* examples show how, after reviewing the information in this book, an existing résumé was improved by one job candidate.

Before

RÉSUMÉ

Name
Address
Pittsburgh, Pennsylvania 15219
(412) 555-0000

WORK HISTORY

Strong sales background with ability to teach and transfer; excellent letter and copy techniques; capability of creating, preparing and articulating complete original presentation; quality of addressing fresh or unusual problems and making opportunities of them.

NOVEMBER 1982 to PRESENT: Classified Manager, The Daily Record, Pittsburgh, PA.   Morning circulation 60,000 daily and 70,000 Sunday. Set up new system for Classified Outside Sales and created phone sales department. Entire new format for section. A broad incentive plan for personnel and creative rates for business contracts and non-business (person to person) advertising. Revenue has more than doubled in less than two years with projected Classified income well over $7,000,000 in 1984.

(continued)

SEPTEMBER 1979 to OCTOBER 1982: Advertising Manager, Times Herald, Pittsburgh, Pennsylvania. Evening circulation 30,000. Involved in all facets of change from hot metal to cold type plus computer start-up and training personnel on use of VDT for ads. Reduced large credit backlog with almost no customer loss and held modest gain in heavy economically depressed area. Set-up total market coverage with 60,000 once-a-week inserts.

JANUARY 1971 to SEPTEMBER 1979: The Philadelphia Evening and Sunday Bulletin, Philadelphia, Pennsylvania. Served as salesman; outside sales supervisor; outside training manager and Phone Advertising Manager. As salesman doubled percentage of field in most assigned areas and was very successful in new sales areas. For several years was responsible for the hiring and training of Classified and Retail ad sales personnel. Was first to use Wats line in phone room and was responsible for computer change over as Phone Ad Manager. Covered major companies, and New York/Philadelphia ad agencies handling recruitment and institutional advertising.

PRIOR: Yellow Page sales; previous time with Bulletin as well as personal ad agency work on West Coast and in Las Vegas.

BUSINESS AWARDS: Philadelphia Bulletin "SALESMAN OF THE YEAR" 1973
Pennsylvania Association of Personnel Services,
"MAN OF THE YEAR" 1977

PERSONAL HISTORY

EDUCATION: Temple University Night Program in Marketing
Penn State Management School

MILITARY: U.S. Army Security Agency and Special Services with two year overseas tour in Germany.

HEALTH: Good

After

NAME
Address
Pittsburgh, Pennsylvania 15219
(412) 555-0000

**EMPLOYMENT
HISTORY**

November 1982
to Present

The Daily Record, Pittsburgh, PA
Classified Manager
Paper has a daily circulation of 60,000 and a Sunday circulation of 70,000.
- Created new system for Classified Outside Sales and set up phone sales department
- Successfully implemented new formation for classified section
- Established broad incentive plan for personnel
- Developed creative rates for business contracts and nonbusiness advertising
- Revenue has more than doubled in less than two years
  Projected classified income for 1984: $7,000,000

September
1979 to
October 1982

Times Herald, Pittsburgh, PA
Advertising Manager
Paper has evening circulation of 30,000
- Involved in all facets of change from hot metal to cold type
- Trained personnel on use of VDT for ads
- Reduced large credit backlog with almost no customer loss; held modest gain in heavy economically depressed area
- Set up total market coverage with 60,000 once-a-week inserts

(continued)

| January 1971 to September 1979 | The Philadelphia Evening Star and Sunday Bulletin |
| | *Sales Supervisor* |

- Served as outside salesman
- Managed phone advertising
- Hired and trained all new personnel in Classified and Retail ad sales
- Covered major companies and New York/Philadelphia ad agencies scheduling recruitment and institutional advertising

BUSINESS AWARDS

| 1977 | Voted "Man of the Year" by the Pennsylvania Association of Personnel Services, Philadelphia, PA |
| 1973 | "Salesman of the Year" Philadelphia Bulletin |

EDUCATION

| 1970 | Temple University Night Program in Marketing Penn State Management School |

REFERENCES   Available on request

MODEL RÉSUMÉS

SEVENTEEN résumés follow, which we classify as "excellent." Use them to help you improve your own résumé. Your final product should be as powerful and eye-pleasing as these samples.

> *Please note:* The size of this book does not allow for the model résumés to appear as one-page formats. We strongly recommend that you follow Rule 47 and keep your résumé to one page in length.

NAME
Address
Bridgeport, Connecticut 06600
203–555–0000

EDUCATION

Emerson College, Boston, Massachusetts
B.S. in Mass Communications
  Television Production
Minor in Psychology
May 1985

**PRE-
PROFESSIONAL
EXPERIENCE**

Production/Film Editor Intern
WPRI—CHANNEL 12—ABC AFFILIATE
Bridgeport, CT
Worked on remote production crew on various locally produced commercials, responsible for lighting, set up and disassembling equipment, running tape, slating and camera assistant. 1984

PM Magazine Producer Intern
WJAR—CHANNEL 10—NBC AFFILIATE
Bridgeport, CT
Responsibilities included setting up shooting locations, researching story ideas, working in conjunction with producers in preproduction and postproduction, remote crew production assistant. 1983

Public Relations/Promotion/Production Intern
WSBE—CHANNEL 36—PUBLIC TELEVISION
Organized and implemented various activities affiliated with fundraiser, direct viewer contact, live studio production assistant. 1981

SPECIAL ACHIEVEMENTS

Corporate training tape concerning Judicial Response for Massachusetts, State Justice System Co-Producer, Director, Editor. 1985

Documentary *Guarded Freedom*, presentation relating to Massachusetts Parole System, which is utilized as a public relations tool for the Massachusetts Parole Board. Producer, director, writer, researcher, and editor. 1984

Music Video, selected original music and creative ideas for presentation of music on videotape, team effort of preproduction, production, and postproduction. 1983

Talk Show *Daybreak*, live on tape, four camera studio production. Producer, director, writer, and researcher. 1983

References available upon request

NAME
Address
Los Angeles, CA 90012

Home: 213-555-0000   Work: 213-555-0000

OBJECTIVE:
Personnel Recruiter/Generalist Position

EXPERIENCE:
February 1981 to Present
Wilson, Fried & Barry, Los Angeles, CA
Assistant to the Office Administrator/Personnel Recruiter

Personnel Responsibilities Include:
— Recruiting, testing, placement, and orientation of new nonlegal staff;
— Maintain personnel records, attendance, and vacation schedules;
— Prepare EEO, OSHA and Workman's Compensation reports;
— Assist in processing of medical claims and act as liaison between insurance carrier and employees for problem claims;
— Employee relations;
— Conduct Exit Interviews of nonlegal staff.

Office Service Responsibilities Include:
— Assist in general management of office operations;
— All maintenance and repairs for the firm;
— Issue and cancel employee identification cards and credit cards;
— Review maintenance agreements, bills and invoices;
— Purchase supplies, equipment, and furniture;
— Office reconstruction, expension, and relocation;
— Prepare various monthly reports;
— Conduct equipment inventory;
— Draft in-house office directory biannually;
— Plan and coordinate firm's Christmas party and annual firm outing;
— Coordinate Lighthouse Drive, Annual Blood Drive, CPR Courses, and Fire Safety Programs.

June 1979 to February 1981
Kirke, Kirke & Associates, Malibu, CA

Hired as Receptionist and promoted to Personnel Assistant after eight months. Duties included benefits administration for over 500 employees. Processing, follow-up and troubleshooting on medical claims. Various projects and general assistance for Personnel Manager as needed.

EDUCATION:
B.A. King's College, Briarcliff Manor, NY, Criminal Justice, 1979.

OBJECTIVE:
Personnel Recruiter/Generalist Position

REFERENCES:
Furnished upon request.

NAME

Home: 612–555–0000   104 Palmer Court
Business: 612–555–0000   St. Paul Minnesota 55149

EXPERIENCE   **Young Presidents' Organization, Inc.** St. Paul, MN
1983 to present   *Seminar Associate, Education Dept.*
(June 1984 to present)
- Responsible for overall planning of twenty educational seminars annually in such areas as: finance, marketing, strategic planning, human resources and specific industry programs. Includes development of new programs, services and educational concepts.
- Manage US $1.2 million annual budget; develop and control individual seminar budgets of + US $50,000.
- Coordinate, implement, and evaluate seminar programs.
- Negotiate contracts with consultants, international conference/convention services and travel organizations.
- Coordinate with various private institutions and government agencies in the development of educational curriculum.
- Interface with United States Embassies worldwide to develop economic, political, and commercial briefings for international programs.
- Plan, implement, and evaluate international programs including Greece, Egypt, Israel, and USSR.

Grant Administration, Education Dept.
(January 1983 to January 1985)
- Supervised, administered, and coordinated International Management Development Program under two-year grant secured from the US Agency for International Development to implement management training programs in seven lesser-developed countries.
- Managed US $.5-million-grant budget; prepared and provided quarterly financial reports to USAID.

- Edited and evaluated program proposals and programmatic reports.
- Interfaced with USAID and member chairman to develop educational curriculum for grant extension.
- Screened member applicants; selected chairmen and participants for management teams.
- Organized and maintained scheduling of overall program agenda.

1982–1983   **Women in Data Processing, Inc.** Minneapolis, MN
Executive Assistant
- Assisted in the planning, development, and implementation of training workshops for human resource managers and data processing professionals.
- Coordinated on-site logistics; negotiated resource contracts; prepared resource biographies.
- Provided liaison services to business and industry, interfacing at all corporate levels.
- Organized department activities, established priorities.
- Recruited, hired, and trained all administrative personnel.

1980–1982   **The Rainbow Room, Rockefeller Center,** NY, NY
Professional Entertainer

EDUCATION   **University of Maryland,** College Park, MD
1975–1979   B.A. in Speech Pathology and Audiology.
Minor in Psychology

NAME
Address
Des Moines, Iowa 50318
515-555-0000

Employment:

July 1985
to Present

Assistant Loan Officer
Des Moines Federal Savings

- Approved consumer loan applications and assisted customers with lending needs and advice.
- As loan collector, used individual approaches to collect loans and assisted customers with debt counseling.
- Prepared written and oral reports for bank management.
- Analyzed customer financial statements for sound loan decisions.
- Chairperson and Coordinator of a Christmas Bazaar for charity. Served two years, raising $2,500.

September 1983 to June 1984

Student Loan Manager
- Calculated student loan portfolio yields. Budgeted loan sales over a four-year period.
- As Student Loan Officer, administered procedures for two million dollar portfolio including loan processing, selling to a secondary market, internal and external reporting, and loan servicing.
- Designed and conducted student loan seminars for community.
- Supervised student loan clerical staff. Demonstrated skills in motivation, training, and delegating.
- Researched and designed an Employee Assistance Program.

June 1982 to September 1983

Management Trainee
- As Management Trainee, became familiar with functions of various departments including Bookkeeping, Customer Service, Accounting, Fed Funds, Collections, IRA, New Accounts, and Installment Loans.

| August 1981 to | *Student Career Advisor Paraprofessional* |
| May 1982 | Career Planning & Placement, St. Ambrose College, Davenport, Iowa |

Education:

| May 1982 | St. Ambrose College, Davenport, Iowa
B.A. Business Concentration: Management
Minor: Psychology
Dean's List, Centennial Scholarship |
| May 1985 | American Institute of Banking
Black Hawk College, Moline, Illinois
Bank Management Skills and Theory Diploma
Foundations of Banking Certificate |

**Activities/
Organizations:**

Professional:

Graduate, Community Leadership School
Credit Women International
Administrative Management Society
Chamber of Commerce
Employees Charity Fund
Delta Sigma Pi Alumni Club

REFERENCES AVAILABLE UPON REQUEST

Name
Address
Madison, Wisconsin 53714
608–555–0000

**WORK
EXPERIENCE:**

Baily Park Press, Inc. , Madison, Wisconsin
MARKETING MANAGER: Social Sciences
November 1983—present
- Responsible for the promotional marketing of all Social Science textbooks, with cumulative annual sales of $20 million and a budget of $400,000.
- Design and direct advertising campaigns.
- Responsible for sales staff education with respect to our product, the competition, and the marketplace.
- Design and implement several 1-week long, in-house training programs for large groups of new sales representatives.
- Set regional and national sales quotas for all introductory-level books; then monitor, analyze, and evaluate personnel, product, and program performance at the end of the sales year.
- Coordinate the design, sales, and marketing strategy for all computer software produced by the College Division.

COLLEGE FIELD EDITOR: Social Sciences and Humanities
June 1982—October 1983
- Coordinated a 13-account territory.
- Manuscript acquisitions and development.
- Instrumental in the contracting of 15 manuscripts with cumulative estimated first year sales in excess of $2 million.
- Directly responsible for a 35% increase in textbook sales.

SALES REPRESENTATIVE: College Division
August 1981—June 1982
- Responsible for a 26-account territory
- Promotion and sale of college textbooks.
- Achieved a 22% increase in territory sales.

Awards:	Northeast Regional Sales Contest: Winner, 1983 Best Product Presentation, National Sales Meeting, 1982 Outstanding Young Men of America, 1982 Awarded for professional achievement, leadership, and community service.

All American Sports, Inc., Waltham, Mass.
September 1978—August 1980
• Designed employee recreational sport tours and sales incentive programs for corporations, schools, and clubs.

EDUCATION:	Brandeis University, Waltham, Mass.
Degree:	Bachelor of Arts, May 1980 Major concentration in ECONOMICS
Honors:	Dean's List Alan B. Saunders Memorial Award for outstanding contributions to the university. Financed 100% of education through scholarships, loans, and employment.

Name
Address
Newport, Rhode Island
314–555–0000

SPECIAL SKILLS
Analytical
Quantitative

CPA Exam   Passed all four sections November 1983 and
               May 1984

Education   M.S., University of Rhode Island, Sept. 1983
               Major: Accounting

               B.S. State University of New York at Buffalo,
                 August 1982
               Major: Business Administration
               Minor: Financial Management

Work   **Staff Accountant,** Taft Inc., Cumberland, RI
Experience   February 1984—Present
               Responsibilities include preparation of individ-
               ual, trust, and corporate tax returns. Other duties
               performed are handling of write-ups, bank
               reconciliations, brokerage statement analysis,
               general ledgers, trial balances, financial state-
               ments, and payroll returns. Used WANG com-
               puter for taxes. Worked with clients on a
               personal basis on behalf of employer.

               Company Representative, Frank Perry Assoc.,
               Buffalo, NY
               November 1981—January 1982
               Coordinated clerical duties as well as guided
               people in their investment opportunities.

               Clerk, Office of Student Affairs
               (School of Management—SUNY at Buffalo)
               September 1980—May 1981
               Responsible for student affairs and performed
               administrative and clerical duties.

Office Assistant, Economics Department
(SUNY at Buffalo) September 1979—May 1980
 ̶ 'sted in departmental administration as well
   ied and collated departmental information.

Comp

Ex

projects using SAS, SPSS and

ie tax preparer; tutoring in
   omics, and related subjects;
   anselor.

   counting position with a major
   concern.

   vailable upon request.

Address • Boston, Massachusetts • 617–555–0000

CAREER OBJECTIVE A challenging position in the field of Public Relations offering ample opportunity for wide exposure and advancement.

EDUCATION **BOSTON UNIVERSITY**
COLLEGE OF COMMUNICATION Boston, MA
B.S., Public Relations, conferred May 1985.
Extensive coursework in the areas of Corporate Public Relations/Public Affairs, and Political Science.

ACADEMIC ACHIEVEMENTS: Dean's Host 1982–1983, Orientation Leader 1983, Boston University Scholarship.
responsibilities include:
- creating and organizing new ways to promote the college's image nationwide.
- principal liaison between the Dean and prospective students/parents.
- coordinate and initiate innovative ways to help new students adjust to campus life.

EXTRACURRICULAR ACTIVITIES: Part-time student employment, Intramural softball.

EXPERIENCE **Massachusetts Fair Share, Boston, MA**
May 1984–Aug. 1984

A major consumer advocate group providing lobbying and community awareness services on a statewide level.
Canvasser
Working as part of a team on a wide spectrum of public issues ranging from toxic waste to auto insurance.
responsibilities include:
- fundraising
- providing community awareness and education
- office work

Wall Street Restaurant & Lounge, Bricktown, NJ
May 1983–Aug. 1983; Dec. 1983–Jan. 1984
Coventry Square Condominium Assoc.,
Lakewood, NJ May 1982–Sept. 1982

REFERENCES Furnished upon request.

NAME
Address
White Plains, NY 10601   914–555–0000

INTERNATIONAL MARKETING/MANAGEMENT EXECUTIVE
With Fortune 100 Multi-National/Multi-Product Company
International Contracts and Agreements
Development of International Marketing and Distribution Channels
Management of Overseas Sales and Service Offices

**employment
record**

1980–present   **SPERRY CORPORATION, ELECTRONIC
SYSTEMS DIVISION, New York, NY
Manager, International Agreements**

Management responsibility for four overseas offices and three domestic offices in the Electronic Systems Division—volume: ten-figure range.

• Management responsibility for seven offices —prepared and administered a multi-million-dollar budget.

• Direct and indirect responsibility for staff of 28 middle and upper management personnel.

• Developed processes and procedures for the appointment process.

• Negotiated international contracts with foreign governments, worldwide, with particular emphasis on the Middle East and Europe.

• Designed and implemented systems and procedures resulting in increased productivity and efficiency in foreign and domestic offices.

• Human resource management responsibilities included in the establishment of relocation guidelines for expatriates and other personnel functions.

(continued)

1970–1980   **BENDIX CORPORATION, INTERNATIONAL
MARKETING OPERATIONS, New York, NY**

Manager, International Contracts

Analyzed, drafted and negotiated major international contracts and agreements in 85
countries.

- Managed a worldwide network of representatives, distributors and dealers (350 in 85
countries).

- Upgraded the quality of representation through
the selection and deletion of representatives/
distributors.

Senior Contracts Administrator

Drafted, negotiated, and administered special
contracts, worldwide.

- Conducted in-depth tax liabilities studies in
local countries, which identified potential tax
problems.

- Liaison between top management in the International Marketing Division, Legal Department
and other departments.

Distributor Development Administrator

Organized the department from inception. Established policy and procedure requirements.
Designed and implemented all internal systems
and procedures. Introduced the use of standard
form agreements resulting in substantial savings
in commission payments and increased controls.

Licensing Specialist

Reviewed existing and investigated potential foreign and domestic licensing agreements. Prepared forecasts and analyses of foreign royalty income plan (multi-million dollar). Investigated potential foreign licensing arrangements, conducted in-depth market analyses and reviewed and evaluated license agreement terms and conditions.

Participated in the design and implementation of a new data processing system for the department.

1969   **EUREKA'S, New York, New York**

Manager

Profit and loss responsibility for a high volume specialized retailing operation in midtown Manhattan.

education   The City University of New York (4.0 Grade Point Average)

references   Personal and business references available on request.

Address
New York, NY 10025
212-555-0000

EDUCATION

MBA. Sept. 1985
Northeastern University, Boston, MA

B.S. in Chemical Engineering. Jan. 1984
State University of New York at Buffalo, Buffalo, NY

EXPERIENCE

Financial Analyst at Burroughs Corporation Eastern Region
Roseland, NJ   June–Dec. 1985
- performed analysis of financial operations on variances between actual and budgeted performances
- compiled and coordinated the equipment orders, revenue, manpower and expense data needed for the 1986 forecasts
- evaluated and ranked districts and branches on their financial performances
- calculated the district and branch managers' bonuses each quarter
- analyzed the financial implication and profitability of proposed business deals
- prepared various report packages for managerial meetings, this requires extensive usage of the B20 (multiplan) and B7900 systems

Internship program at ARCO Metals Company—Anaconda Brass Division
Buffalo, NY   June–Sept. 1984
- determined the volume of process water discharged daily and the amount of metal in it
- performed tests on assorted discharge waters to obtain the amount of oil and grease present
- conducted research on the U.S.E.P.A. regulations on the effluent and made necessary recommendations to management

COMPUTER SKILLS

PASCAL, FORTRAN, BASIC

REFERENCES: Will be submitted upon request

Name
Address
New York, New York 10022
212-555-0000

Experience

The Churchill School for Learning Disabled Students, New York, NY
Teacher. 1984 to Present. Program individualized education plans for state Committee on Handicapped. Evaluate student performance, design and implement daily work plans. Coordinate peer review program. Report student progress in conference with parents and specialists. Edit student newspaper.

Hinckley Lake Camp, Inc. for Learning Disabled Students, New York, NY
Administrative Assistant. 1984 to Present. Correspond with prospective employees. Organize all information on 120 campers. Assemble learning material for all campers. Operate within limited budget.

The Cambridge Montessori School,
Cambridge, MA
Special Services Teacher. 1980–1984. Assessed academic needs of learning disabled students in Resource Room. Designed and implemented individualized education plans. Directed and unified efforts of staff and parents. Interviewed parents of prospective students.

Bradley Hospital for Emotionally Disturbed Children, E. Providence, RI
Project Director. 1979–1980. Initiated statistical analysis of behavior modification program. Coordinated work of psychologists and teachers. Presented findings of full staff to psychologists, teachers, and Brown Psychology Department.

Psychiatric Institute of Washington, DC
Intern. Summer, 1978. Conferred with psychologists, psychiatrists, and nurses on programming behavior modification for childrens' unit. Assessed and recorded daily progress of children. Managed crisis situations.

(continued)

Education	**Brown University, Providence, RI.** AB Honors Psychology, 1979
	Honors Thesis tested new theory on autistic behavior. Research accepted by Bradley Hospital and Brown University Psychology Department.
	Coursework included Psychology, Comparative Literature, and French.
References	On request

NAME
Address
Livingston, NJ 07039   201-555-0000

Objective:	Advertising/sales promotion position with challenging creative and administrative responsibilities.
Professional Skills:	Effect corporate marketing goals and new product introductions through advertising and sales promotion, to a national and international audience of professionals, trade associations and consumers.
	Conceptualize and write copy for print, radio, and collateral materials, including sales kits, brochures, direct mail, flip charts, point-of-purchase displays.
	Develop and monitor a $2 million advertising and sales promotion budget, establishing cost guidelines and controls to meet individual department budget parameters.
	Counsel the corporate advertising agency in the creation and implementation of national advertising campaign, including media selection and planning.
	Purchase outside creative vendor services to supplement in-house capabilities, evaluating all phases of production from inception to distribution of printed materials.
Business Experience:	Manager, Advertising and Sales Promotion Royal Insurance Companies 12/81–Present
	Sales Promotion Coordinator Continental Insurance Companies 12/80–12/81
	Senior Copywriter American International Group 12/77–12/80
	Copywriter Mercury Advertising, Ltd. 6/75–12/77

(continued)

Copywriter
D.F.C. Inc.
Freelance
Illustrations for consumer, business and employee publications; written articles for humor magazines.
2/72–6/75

Education: Bachelor of Science, Journalism, 1971
Southern Illinois University, Carbondale, IL

Further studies in advertising at
The School of Visual Arts, New York City

References: Furnished on request.

NAME

Address, Rockville, Maryland 20850   301–555–0000

CONTROLLER/FINANCIAL EXECUTIVE

Extensive background with small and medium-sized multi-division companies in domestic and international operations. Skilled in projections, analyses and P&L responsibility. Strong in internal auditing, cash and budget management and insurance negotiation. In-depth knowledge of operations management and joint ventures.

SELECTED ACHIEVEMENTS

- Changed a deficit position to a surplus of over $1,000,000 within a period of two-and-a-half years by converting the accounting system to EDP and establishing a cash management system.
- Decreased interest expense over $100,000 annually through loan consolidation, controlled borrowing and implementation of an effective cash budget.
- Reduced payroll 20% by evaluating, reorganizing and standardizing operating procedures.
- Generated turnover reduction to 10% by initiating a profit-sharing plan and improving benefits programs. Employee morale was greatly improved and better qualified personnel were attracted and retained.
- Reduced audit fees more than $50,000 annually by redesigning the chart of accounts and organizing in-house audit assistance programs.
- Cut annual insurance premiums by $100,000 through installation of comprehensive loss control programs.
- Recovered $1.5 million excess payments for liability insurance premiums and commissions paid in earlier years through review, analysis and renegotiation of policies.

(continued)

NAME

BUSINESS AFFILIATIONS

Omega Corp.   Controller/Chief Financial Officer
American Export   Controller/Chief Financial Officer
Caster & Sons, Inc.   Treasurer/Corporate Secretary
Kobel & Floyd   Controller/Chief Accountant
Middletown Hospital   Operations Manager

EDUCATION

Brooklyn College   B.S. Accounting (Cum Laude)
NYU   EDP
School of World Trade   International Trade Management

Address   Washington, DC   202-555-0000

CAREER OBJECTIVE	To pursue a career in the field of marketing and/or advertising fully utilizing business education, experience, and creative skills.

EDUCATION   B.B.A., Marketing   *May 1985*
George Washington University, Washington, DC

Areas of Academic Concentration:
• Advertising
• Retailing Management
• Marketing Research
• Consumer Behavior
• Sales and Sales Management
• Personnel Management

SPECIAL PROJECTS
• Prepared a situation analysis for a widely distributed product
• Devised a marketing plan for a newly developed product
• Collected and analyzed primary and secondary research data to determine readership response to advertising in the George Washington University newspaper
• Competed regionally in an advertising campaign for Burger King
• Conceived of and assisted in the implementation of a new venture project in retailing

AFFILIATIONS
• Member of the American Marketing Association
• Member of the American Advertising Federation
• Member of the International Thespian Society
• Pollwatcher for student elections

(*continued*)

EXPERIENCE   **SALES ASSISTANT**   *5/84-Present*
Peterson's, Washington, DC
  • Produced maximized sales through compre-
    hensive merchandising and maintenance of
    selling floor
  • Executed sales promotional efforts
  • Prepared merchandise for effective inventory
    control
  • Analyzed weekly and monthly status reports
  • Built strong channels of communication with
    upper management

Advertising Intern   *2/83-3/83*
Hammer & Lloyd, Washington, DC
  • Assisted in the collection of SMRB data
  • Constructed demographic profiles for poten-
    tial target markets
  • Demonstrated general office skills

Merchandising and Sales Assistant   *6/83-8/83*
The Jean's Place, Toms River, NJ
  • Created window and fixture displays for the
    previewing of merchandise
  • Assumed managerial responsibilities of staff
    supervision and opening/closing of store
  • Maintained operation and reconciliation of
    cash register

Additional experience as an independent marketing representative (Ésprit) and a relief receptionist (dental office).

NAME
Address
New York, NY 10023
212-555-0000

CAREER
OBJECTIVE:
To obtain a position in the financial industry that will lead to a position as a senior financial analyst.

EDUCATION:
Drexel University, Philadelphia, PA
MBA—December 1984
Concentration: Finance

State University of New York at Albany
Bachelor of Science—December 1984
Concentration: Business and Marketing
Education

EMPLOYMENT HISTORY:

March 1982–
Sept. 1983
The Geon Corp.
New York, NY
Research Department

Research Assistant/Pharmaceutical Industry
Responsibilities included interviewing of management teams for the purpose of analyzing financial data needed to obtain the profit ratios of targeted pharmaceutical companies. The information determined whether a company was to be put on our preferred to "buy or sell" list. In addition, responsible for the presentation of this information to management and making recommendations based on the obtained data.

May 1982–
Aug. 1983
Registered Representative
Limited selling experience

Jan. 1982–
May 1982
Teaching Assistant for Business Law
State University of New York at Albany

Organized and conducted business law classes as well as supervise study programs.

Peer Advisor
State University of New York at Albany

Provided assistance with the construction of individual academic programs for students.

(continued)

May 1981– Sept. 1981	**Loan Processor/Commercial Loan Division** Banker's Trust Company, New York, NY
	Responsibilities included the organization and maintenance of loan transactions, and the utilization of in-house computer for data validation and other functions.
AFFILIATIONS:	Registered Representative Series 7 (New York) MBA Society, Member American Vocational Association, Member
REFERENCES:	Available upon request.

NAME
Address   Garden City, NY   516-555-0000

EXPERIENCE: *FOUNDATION FOR THE*
TAYLOR BALLET INC., NYC (1983 . . .)
Marketing Assistant

Direct Mail:
- Research, develop and implement installation of new on-line computer system for ticket buyer and donor lists
- Coordinate mailing list acquisition for large mailings and maintenance of computerized customer list
- Analyze data and report on response statistics relating to direct mail
- Develop and implement computer programs for subscriber and donor lists
- Train personnel to use computer

Merchandising:
- Manage promotional merchandise by keeping inventory of stock
- Establish contacts nationally to create merchandise boutiques in theaters and retail stores for promotional and profit purposes
- Work with merchandise supplier and concessionaires to update inventory and develop merchandise
- Assist in management of New York boutique

Playbill Preparation:
- Prepare all information needed for house programs nationally
- Edit and proofread all copy until final stages of printing
- Organize use of editorial space in programs

Ticket Sales:
- Correlate comparative statistics relating to subscription and single ticket sales
- Handle customer relations

(continued)

General Responsibilities:
- Supervise interns and volunteers
- Coordinate production of graphics material
- Track marketing expenditures and prepare budget reports
- Assess and allocate marketing cash flow
- Coordinate national tour sponsors regarding content and format of ads and supply support materials for promotion

PRIOR EXPERIENCE:

THE BELLEVUE HOUSE, BLOCK ISLAND, RI (summer 1982) Inn Manager

PUBLIC DEFENDER SERVICE, WASHINGTON, DC (spring 1982) Student Investigator

ROBINSON'S DEPARTMENT STORE, NEWPORT, CA (summer 1981) Salesperson

LORD & TAYLOR DEPARTMENT STORE, NORTHBROOK, IL (fall 1979) Salesperson

EDUCATION:

*COLORADO COLLEGE
B.A. in Business/Economics and minor in Dance (1983)*

NORTHWESTERN UNIVERSITY (fall 1979)

NAME

Address   **East Brunswick, New Jersey**   **201-555-0000**

EXPERIENCE

Director of Marketing
Fearon Corp., Piscataway, NJ   **1985**

Developed and managed marketing of multimedia software through a network of agents, mail-order distributors and retail outlets. Planned and supervised advertising/promotion, direct-response and telemarketing strategies. Prepared budgets, P&L studies, and conducted market research. Directed trade show operations and deliver presentations at industry meetings.

Results: Sales were increased at an average annual rate of 11 percent in the past four years. This was accomplished by: increasing salesforce performance by 16 percent in one year, offering premiums and discounts, increasing use of mail-order distributors by 40 percent, and opening distribution to overseas markets, i.e., Japan, South Korea, and Saudi Arabia. U.S. markets were expanded through more advertising, direct mail, promotion, and new packaging concepts.

Director of Marketing Services
Deko Division, Hamilton, NJ   **1982-1985**

In charge of catalog production, promotion, advertising, and direct mail. Supervised customer service staff. Established monthly newsletter for dealers and reps. Wrote news releases and secured product reviews.

Director, Special Services
County of Sussex, Branchville, NJ   **1975-1982**

Wrote and administered Federal and State grants to represent the interests of the handicapped in areas of transportation, housing, employment, and recreation. Organized publicity, special events, news conferences and public appearances. Established series of seminars and workshops to educate legislators and citizens groups.

(continued)

Administrative Assistant to New York State Senator
Albany, NY   **1974–1975**
Head of staff to Sen. James McFarland, 59th District. Conducted research and prepared treatments for proposed legislation. Speechwriting and campaign responsibilities. Managed media and constituent relations. Published monthly newsletter, and wrote press releases, as well as public service communications.

Placement Coordinator
Bethany College, Buffalo, NY   **1973–1974**
Developed and directed an internship program for Media Department. Placed over 150 students with radio/television stations, public relations firms, and advertising agencies on a work/study basis.

EDUCATION

State University of New York at Buffalo, B.A. History, 1972. SUNY at Buffalo, Grant Writing and Management Courses, 1976.

MEMBERSHIPS

DMMA—Direct Mail Marketing Association
NAVA—National Audio Visual Association
AMP—Association of Media Producers

NAME
Address
Ithaca, New York 14850
616–555–0000

Career Objective

To obtain an interesting and challenging career in the area of personnel management of labor relations utilizing skills in staff training and development, public relations and administration.

Education

Graduate and Continuing Studies: 21 hours
Towson State University, Baltimore, MD

Related Courses:
• Personnel Management
• Labor Economics and Relations
• Industrial Psychology
• Individual Intelligence Testing (Graduate)
• Projective Personality Assessment Techniques I and II (Graduate)

Bachelor of Science, Psychology, May 1980
State University College of Cortland, Cortland, NY

Professional Experience

Assistant to Coordinator of On-Campus Programming
Towson State University, August 1980–June 1981

• Researched necessary information for administrators of Residence Life, and implemented a filing system for accessible means of retrieval.
• Developed and instructed a formal training course for para-professional Residence Advisors.
• Evaluated and reviewed the performance of Residence Advisor trainees.
• Established and published:

Monthly newsletter to Off-Campus University students concerning University policies and services and tenant rights and responsibilities.

Bi-weekly newsletter distributed to aid and support the program facilitators in the residence halls.

(continued)

- Reporter and publisher of weekly newsletter composed of University and Non-University activities.
- Assisted in the development of programming budget for On-Campus activities and programs.

Residence Life Experience

Resident Assistant, State University College at Cortland, August 1978–May 1980

Directly responsible for educational and social development of 36 undergraduate students. Reponsibilities included peer counseling, discipline and student behavior, educational and social programming, conflict mediation and other administrative tasks necessary in creating a sense of community. Planned activities to assist the evolvement of staff cohesion., Involved in the observation, interview and selection of Resident Assistants.

References

Available upon request.

RÉSUMÉ CHECKLIST

RATE your résumé's effectiveness. Include comments as to how an area could be improved. Score your résumé based on the following scale:

1 = Excellent   2 = Satisfactory   3 = Needs Work

Personal Résumé Critique

AREA	SCORE	COMMENTS/IMPROVEMENTS
Overall appearance		
Readability		
Layout		
Consistency		
Length		
Relevance		
Writing style		
Action-oriented		
Specificity		
Employment		
Education		
Accomplishments		
Completeness		
Effectiveness		
	Total:	

Score: 14-17 Your current résumé is excellent; don't make unnecessary changes.

18-21 You have a good résumé; target in on areas for improvement; work on making it great.

22+ You need to reevaluate your résumé as it is now. Why not rewrite it before you send it out again?

Résumé Worksheet

Name: _____

Address: _____

City, State, Zip Code: _____

Job Objective (See Rule 3): _____

_____

_____

Work Experience

    Job Title: _____

    Employer 1: _____

    Address: _____

    Dates of Service: _____

    Responsibilities: _____

_____

_____

Résumé Worksheet (*continued*)

Job Title: _____

Employer 2: _____

Address: _____

Dates of Service: _____

Responsibilities: _____

_____

_____

Job Title: _____

Employer 3: _____

Address: _____

Dates of Service: _____

Responsibilities: _____

_____

_____

Memberships: _____

Education
Name of School 1: _____

Location: _____

Degree: _____

Major/Minor: _____

Date of Graduation: _____

Honors/Activities: _____

_____

Name of School 2: _____

Location: _____

Degree: _____

Major/Minor: _____

Date of Graduation: _____

Honors/Activities: _____

Special Skills: _____

_____

Selected Accomplishments: _____

_____

_____

Continuing Education Courses: _____

_____

_____

A LAST WORD OF ADVICE

WE have offered you every trick we know for developing a powerful and effective résumé.

Some people will tell you that résumés are unnecessary. Don't let them fool you. Even if an employer doesn't read your résumé, he/she will want to be assured that you have one. The résumé's current popularity has transformed it into a mainstay of modern business. A résumé that projects a positive, professional image will represent you well.

Get the résumé...get the interview...get the job!

Good luck.